CONTENTS

THE PERFORMANCE PRINCIPLE

MACKENZIE KYLE

PERFORMANCE PRINCIPLE

A Practical Guide to
Understanding Motivation
in the Modern Workplace

Figure.1

Vancouver / Berkeley

Cataloguing data available from Library and Archives Canada
ISBN 978-1-927958-65-0 (pbk.)
ISBN 978-1-927958-66-7 (ebook)
ISBN 978-1-927958-67-4 (pdf)

Editing by Barbara Pulling
Copy editing by Eva van Emden
Interior design by Ingrid Paulson
Author photograph by MNP
Printed and bound in Canada by Friesens
Distributed in the U.S. by Publishers Group West

Figure 1 Publishing Inc.
Vancouver BC Canada
www.figure1pub.com

PREFACE

IN SEPTEMBER 1983, I started my second year of studying sciences at university. My courses comprised predominantly math, chemistry, and physics, but for my one elective I chose a psychology course, in the hope that it would add very little to my workload.

In one of the first classes, I watched a short film documenting some guy named B. F. Skinner working with a severely physically and mentally disabled young girl. The girl was about four years old, and due to her challenges she had never walked. Over the course of five hours, using only a clothesline and ice cream, Skinner taught the little girl to walk on her own.

I was mesmerized. What magic was this Skinner fellow working? And how could I learn to do it? My throwaway elective soon became my favorite course, and that class kicked off my lifelong fascination with understanding why people do the things they do. Over the years, I learned just how much real science there was related to this topic and I discovered the large body of knowledge that can assist us with what we sometimes refer to as performance management.

So, why write a book about it? As the old saying goes, "In theory, theory and practice are the same. In practice, they are not." During my consulting career, I've had the opportunity to translate elements of the body of knowledge about performance management into practical tools and techniques that I, and the teams I've worked with, have used to help people and organizations improve their situation with regard to real problems. The translation from theory to practice is not always straightforward, but this book is intended to provide some useful perspective on how to make that transition. Written as a novel, this book offers a realistic depiction of some situations we all face and illustrates in a practical way how to apply some basic principles to improve them.

Mackenzie Kyle
Vancouver, British Columbia
September 2015

ONE

CHANGES

MY PHONE BUZZED. It was Jake. Again.

When r u coming home?

People today don't like to talk. We text, we tweet, we BBM, we Facebook, we iMessage. If we're really old school, we send each other emails. These days, that's pretty much the technological equivalent of sending a letter via the post office. But we don't call each other. Maybe it has something to do with the fact that an actual conversation takes more time than we think we have.

I sound like a grumpy old man when I say that, but first of all, forty-three is far from old, and secondly, it's really more of an observation than a complaint. I'm not saying that all these new ways of connecting are inferior to talking; in many circumstances, I think they lead to *more* communication, rather than less.

Case in point: my teenage son. Jake is fourteen. When I was that age, my friends and I would only grunt in the general direction of our dads if we happened to find ourselves in the same room. And generally we'd avoid being in the same room.

Now, I text with Jake ten times a day. With my fifteen-year-old daughter, Sarah, it's probably twice that. Maybe it's not talking, but it's a lot better than grunting.

My phone buzzed again.

?

The downside of all this communication? Sometimes there's guilt attached. I texted him back.

I'll tell u in 20 min

IN THE MORE than ten years I've been working for him, Ralph Borsellino has remained almost irritatingly youthful. The stress of being the CEO of a ten-billion-dollar company apparently agrees with him; if anything, he looks younger today than he did when I first knew him as the president of a small manufacturing operation in Oregon. Although I didn't know it back then, his decision to turn me into a project manager would change the course of my career, cause my hairline to recede, and tie my rise in the corporate world to his. And ultimately, lead to those texts from my son.

I can't say that I actually like Ralph, but I do respect him. Even though he can be a real bastard.

"I don't get it, Will," he complained as he stared at me across the table. "This isn't a step forward. This isn't even a step sideways. It's Hyler. Yes, we still own the place, but it's hardly a jewel in the Mantec crown. Plus, you've done that. And it's in Oregon. Why do you want to go there?" Ralph's rise to CEO at Mantec had long since meant his relocation to Chicago, which is where I seemed to spend a lot of my time.

"First of all," I told him, "I know you have a hard time remembering this, but Oregon is actually my home. Once in a while I even get to visit. It's nice. Turns out that's where my family lives."

I watched the inevitable eye roll. The word "family" does not make a regular appearance in conversations with Ralph; he believes the whole concept is an inconvenient infringement on all those extra hours in the day when you should really be working.

"Second," I continued, "Hyler is not the same place it was when you left. They're building a whole range of products now. It's close to a $500-million-a-year operation."

"And shrinking by the minute," he said. "It's got technology problems, a bad union environment, and a range of products the American public isn't so keen on these days. And what the public does want to buy, we should be making in one of our plants in India. Or Indonesia. If you go back to Hyler, you might be the guy who ends up turning out the lights on the whole operation. Is that what you want for the next stage of your career?"

That part was true. The downturn in 2008 hit the recreation industry pretty hard, and more than a decade of significant growth at the Hyler plant had first gone flat, then backward. For Mantec overall, Hyler's fortunes were only a blip. The corporation had shed its underperforming forestry division and most of its consumer products businesses well before the crash and had gotten heavily into oil and gas, not to mention various industrial products supporting that very same industry. Hyler had become the black sheep of the corporate family, and lately it had been transforming into the redheaded stepchild from three marriages ago.

But as I told Ralph, Hyler was also home. And that was a place I hadn't really been in a long while.

I guess all this requires some explanation.

A long time ago, in a place far away from Chicago, a young man named Will Campbell came to fame within the Mantec world by bringing a new product to market for the company. This product, a unique take on windsurfing and sailing, proved to be a major hit for the corporation and propelled a guy named Ralph Borsellino from president of a relatively small division in Oregon to a VP job for the West Coast division and eventually to the top job in the whole damn company. Some still say Ralph "Windsailored" his way to the top. But not to his face.

The product propelled Will along quite the path as well, although a different one. Based on his success with the Windsailor, Will started going from plant to plant in the Mantec world, taking on increasingly large and complex projects while developing a reputation for delivering results. He gradually branched out from new product launches to implementing IT systems, and then into the realm of "operations improvement." He was trained in the philosophies of W. Edwards Deming and statistical quality control. He became a black belt in Lean. He learned all about Kanban and Agile. He turned into a certified performance improvement guru, and his project work expanded to include fixing just about any serious problem that existed across the Mantec universe.

Ten years passed, and Will woke up one day to discover that he had super-elite frequent flyer status on four airlines, that he was a President's Club member with six different hotel chains, and that he no longer knew his wife or his kids.

Sounds dramatic, right? I know. It's not 100 percent true, but then when you see the movie version of my life, you'll find the actor who plays me is also much better-looking than I am.

What *is* true is that ten years had gone by for me, I'd become a bit of a company-wide "expert" in project management and all sorts of philosophies of improvement, and I'd spent too much time traveling and away from my family. It wasn't all bad, of course. We've had some great family vacations on all those travel miles, and with technology the way it is, I've been able to organize a fair bit of my life working out of my home office. I've been able to do things like walk my kids to school more often than parents who work a regular eight-to-five job, and that flexibility has been worth something.

Still, you can spend only so much time in airports before you start to go a little loony. The family card I was playing with Ralph was certainly part of the reason I wanted to go back to the Hyler division. But there was more to it from a professional perspective.

Ten years ago, I'd accidentally come across some ideas about how to make things happen. As the saying goes, do a good job and you'll be rewarded with more work. I had become a lightning rod for the various improvement theories the company wanted to try— Total Quality Management, Six Sigma, and fifty other variations on business process reengineering, all of them coming "just in time." I'd used my project management skills to implement these ideas in a number of our operations around North America and in Asia. I'd trained literally thousands of our employees in how to apply these methods in their daily life at work.

In the process, I'd started to feel more like an evangelist preaching a spiritual state of mind than someone implementing practical management techniques. I was seeing less and less connection between what I was doing and the actual results we were getting. Even weirder was that I seemed to be the only one who noticed this.

So, in addition to being home with my family, I wanted to get out of what felt increasingly like a snake oil sales racket and back to a real job. Of course, I didn't tell Ralph that last part.

Ralph let loose a dramatic sigh and looked toward the heavens. "If you want to travel less, then come to Chicago. You don't need to move to a backwater."

I tried not to scoff. "Head office people do not travel less, Ralph. The only people in this company who travel more than I do are you and your executive VPs. Plus, you've got nothing useful for me to do here. I want to be out in the operation somewhere, working in the business. I'm not a head office type of guy."

For a moment, I thought I saw a glimmer of empathy in Ralph's eyes. Perhaps he felt a certain nostalgia for being out in the field, having a hands-on role in running a plant, actually making a product...

"Will, you're an idiot," he said. Maybe not the kind of glimmer I'd thought. "But only about your career. Otherwise, you've done some great stuff for Mantec. You've earned the right, at least temporarily, to be a career idiot. I can give you a year back at the Hyler operation. But at the end of the year, things are either back on track, or you're the project manager for moving the operation over-seas and shutting the plant down. Personally, I think that's exactly where we're going. But we'll need someone to do that right."

Seven minutes later I was hailing a cab for O'Hare. I texted my son.

Home in six hours

I got a reply in about five seconds.

4 how long?

I thought for a second before I texted.

4 good

I hoped I wasn't lying.

TWO

HOME FOR THE PROBLEM DAYS

RAIN. WE GET a lot of that in the Pacific Northwest. It's not as if I don't have experience with it. But when you're embarking on what you hope is the next great stage of your career, and you're nervous that maybe you've just made a huge mistake, rain can be a real downer.

I watched the fat drops squash themselves on my windshield as I waited to exit the airport parking garage. I thought about how I'd already lied to my son. I'd told him I'd be home in six hours, but that turned out to be how long my flight was delayed departing O'Hare. Traveling through Chicago was something I wasn't going to miss in my new role.

It was already well after midnight. Since the chances of any of my family staying up to greet me were slim, I decided to take a detour by the Hyler plant on the way to the house.

One of the things I've always loved about the plant is that it's got a twenty-acre lake on the property. The lake is owned by the company, and we use it to test some of the recreational water products we make. But mostly it creates a feeling of calm in the midst of a bustling manufacturing facility. These days, "formerly bustling" might be a better way to put it.

When I worked at the plant ten years ago, Hyler was running three shifts a day, seven days a week, producing small boats, sails, and my personal favorite, the Windsailor. Since then, the plant had expanded its operations significantly, both in scale and in the scope of its products. But the start of the recession in 2008 had changed that. As I drove by the main office and parked in front of Lake Hyler, the place was dark. The only things in the plant at that time of night were the ghosts of better days.

The rain had eased off to a light drizzle, which in the Pacific Northwest we think of as "clearing up." I got out of my car and walked down to the edge of the water. The dark plant, the dark lake, and my jet lag took me to a dark place in my mind. Hyler's rise and current slump mirrored how I felt about my own career.

I'd spent the last ten years going from operation to operation making things happen, and ostensibly making things better. But I'd become increasingly focused on the things that didn't get better. Or that got better for a while, and then went back to how they always had been. It felt like these failures were outnumbering the successes. And it all seemed to come down to the people. They would start off doing things the new, better way, but once the excitement of the change had passed, or maybe more importantly once I left town, they slid back into their old ways. The gains in productivity we'd seen fizzled out. Dramatically better production and reduced accident downtime returned to normal.

I picked up a rock and skipped it across the black water. For all my fancy-sounding projects and all the big changes I'd implemented, I didn't feel like I was really making a difference. I wasn't changing the *people*.

"WELL, WELL, the prodigal son returns!"

It was as if I had stepped out of a time machine. One that was a little screwed up, maybe, in that everyone looked as if they'd aged ten years, so really, more of a situation machine...over time... you know what I mean.

Sitting around the table was the group I thought of as my old team. Some of them worked for me back when I was at Hyler full-time, some had been colleagues, and one was my old boss. They reminded me of a familiar old sweater—a little threadbare, maybe with the hint of a musty odor, out of style, but still very comfortable. While I'd been off traveling the Mantec world for the last ten years, they'd been riding the highs and lows of things back here at home. We'd all kept in touch. But for some reason I was feeling a bit odd sitting at the table. That wasn't working with my sweater analogy, but I didn't have time to resolve my metaphorical misalignment.

"Welcome back!" Stu Barnes greeted me with an enthusiastic handshake. "What the hell happened to your hair?"

There was laughter among the group. I shrugged. "I only wear it this way to be cool—bald is the hip look these days. I can't believe you haven't shaved your own head." Stu, the VP of operations at Hyler, had been my boss and mentor from my earliest days there. Although he must have been close to sixty-five, the bastard still sported a thick head of hair, with only a few patches of gray.

"Luckily, you've got just the perfect fat head to make the look work." That was Amanda Payton, the vp of it. Amanda had been on the career fast track, a bit like me, until she'd decided that the travel and time away from the family wasn't quite worth it. It took me a little longer to figure that out.

Also around the table was Mark Goldman, the director of human resources, who'd just been an hr analyst during my time at Hyler. Sheila Chan was now the vp of engineering. Luigi Delgarno was still there as the director of manufacturing, though I was surprised he hadn't retired long ago. Alice Sorensen from accounting and finance, and Leslie Frame, the vp of sales and marketing, rounded out the group. There were more comments, catcalls, and general expressions of skepticism that I was still gainfully employed, surprise at my early release from prison, and speculation about my questionable ancestry before everyone settled down to business.

"I can see by your comments that I've already gained the respect of the team," I told the group. I had to admit, it felt really good to be back. For about three minutes. "ok, guys, you know why I'm here," I said, "so lay it on me—what's our situation?"

There was a moment of uncomfortable silence as everyone looked around the table at each other. Finally, Amanda spoke. "Actually, we're not quite sure why you're here. We all thought Stu was going to be taking the job when Jim Flemming left."

Stu held up his hands, palms outward. "Not that I wanted it. I don't fancy myself in the role of grim reaper."

Alice said, "We're guessing that head office sending you in means we're going to shut everything down that much sooner."

"Shut everything down?" I asked. "Where is that coming from?"

Amanda sighed. "C'mon, Will, you know how things are going. The recession kicked the crap out of the recreation industry, us included. We know it's just a matter of time before everything we make is moved offshore. You've been the special projects guy for ten years. You're here to wrap things up."

"It's no big secret," Luigi added. "We're a manufacturing plant in America. Nobody does that anymore."

Stu shrugged. "We're just happy it's you who's coming in to do it, Will. It's gonna hurt, but better that it's one of our own."

I looked around the room, feeling like the veterinarian who's been summoned on a house call to put down the family cat. "Guys," I protested, "that is not at all what I'm here to do. My job—our job—is to help make Hyler viable again, not close it down." I paused for a minute and glanced at the faces around the table. "How bad is it?"

It wasn't great. As Ralph had outlined, there were issues with production and efficiency, issues with product sales, and issues with delivery times on the products Hyler did sell. And a union problem: grievances, tension, mistrust, and an all-round deteriorating relationship.

I started to tune out as the details of the latest union problem were discussed. I tuned back in again when Stu said, "The bottom line is, if we take this grievance to the next step, we're going to have a strike on our hands." He folded his arms and stared at the paper in front of him on the conference table. "Quite frankly, maybe that's what we should do."

Amanda did not agree. "Are you nuts? A strike? Right now? That's all head office would need to shut us down for good! They're just looking for an excuse." She suddenly remembered I was in the room. "Uh, I mean, I know what you said a minute ago and all, Will, but that's the way it feels sometimes..."

"Maybe head office is right," Stu persisted. "Personally, this union situation has me thinking that offshoring everything we do would be a pretty good idea."

In the past, Stu was always the guy I turned to for sensible advice and he was a positive influence on every situation. He was the last person I'd have expected to make a comment like that.

"Stu, that seems a bit extreme," I said. "Is it really that bad?"

I LOVE MY WIFE. Not in a starry-eyed, I'm-seventeen-and-still-in-love-after-three-weeks kind of way, but more in the been-married-for-nineteen-years-two-teenagers-pets-work-and-family-angst-and-I-still-can't-wait-to-get-home-to-see-her kind of way. I won't go into the details of the mushy stuff that somehow remains strong after all this time, but I will say there is no one I want to see more after a day like the one I'd just had.

I slumped into one of the kitchen chairs. "Do we have any Scotch?" I asked.

Jenny rolled her eyes. "You only drink Scotch when you're trying to be dramatic."

"Good point," I said. "Vodka would be much more effective."

For a moment Jenny looked concerned. "That bad?"

I sighed. "Only if you believe the management team, and there's no reason why I shouldn't. They do have a vested interest in the future of Hyler."

"Hey, Dad, what's up?" Jake sauntered into the kitchen and plunked himself down across the table from me. "How was the first day back?"

"How do you feel about Indonesia?"

He gave me a puzzled look. "I don't get it."

"You don't get it because you're an idiot." Sarah appeared on Jake's heels, texting intently and editorializing, as she normally does.

"Hi, honey," I said. She continued to stroll, text, ignore me, and provide commentary.

"Dad's talking about Indonesia because that's where he's going to move all the work that Hyler does, after he fires everyone and closes down the plant. And since there won't be any more jobs here, we'll all be moving to Indonesia or some other crazy country where we can be sweatshop laborers and work with eight-year-olds fourteen hours a day so that Dad's boss in Chicago can get paid ten million dollars a year." She looked up at me and smiled, her eyes bright with sarcasm. "Isn't that right, Daddy?"

"What makes you say that?" I asked her.

"Duh, Dad. It doesn't take a rocket scientist to figure it out. Everyone at school has been talking about it for months. Most of the parents work at the plant, and everyone has just been waiting for the hatchet man to show up. That's you." A look of actual concern crept across her face. "When that plant closes, this place is going to suck."

Jake made no attempt to hide his worry at her words. "That's not what you're doing, is it, Dad?"

I shook my head, trying to convey complete confidence in my words. "Of course not, Jake. Don't be silly. I'm back here to lead this division, and I'm leading it back into the black, not across the ocean."

Sarah grimaced. "Dad, that is a terrible metaphor."

I nodded. "I agree. But then I'm not back here to be the metaphor king."

"Time to eat," Jenny said, and we transferred our hungry selves to the dining room table.

Later, Jenny and I lay in bed with the lights out. "Really, how bad is it?" she asked. I couldn't see what she was doing, but I was staring intently at the dark ceiling. The evening's conversation had deteriorated into platitudes, broad assurances, and a visit to Google Maps so the kids could see exactly where Indonesia was.

I sighed dramatically to make up for the fact that she couldn't see my face. "It's not good, honey, not good. We've got our traditional American workers, who are relatively expensive and relatively unproductive, a union that has become very powerful and doesn't seem to recognize how bad things are, a management group that hates the union and blames it for all the problems, and an economy that isn't keen on buying anything we make. We're kind of screwed on every front."

Jenny was silent for so long I thought maybe she had gone to sleep. Finally she said, "I don't really want to move to Indonesia, honey." A few minutes after that, I could tell from her breathing she was asleep. Me, I lay awake for most of the night, thinking about how much I didn't want to move, either.

THREE

THE RETURN OF MARTHA

I DON'T NEED people's company these days, and I don't much enjoy it, either. I've spent lots of time with people in my life, and when you get to my stage of the game, you don't want to waste any of the time you have left. I've still got plenty going on in this wrinkled old head, plenty to sort out, and that means the person I want to spend most of my time with is me.

Most people oblige me by not dropping by for a casual chat, and I help them feel better about their decision by playing the part of the grumpy old lady when they do come to see me. It's a situation that works well for all of us. But there are exceptions, and birthdays bring out people's tendency to invade my private space in the worst way. Granted, it's a big deal to have someone in the family pass the hundred-year mark, and this year I turned 102. But really, am I all that different than I was at 101? Or even when I was a spring chicken of 81? I like to think not, though try and tell that to my daughters. Or grandkids. Or, well, all of the relatives out there, of which I seem to have accumulated many. They seem to think I'm some kind of good luck charm. And if they come to pay me homage, maybe it'll remind God that we're related, that they're treating me right, and so they should live a long time too.

Or maybe they just want my money, though there's less of that around than there used to be. Who expects to live past a hundred years? I got good value for my dough, though. I saw a lot of this planet before the thought of another four-hour delay at LAX, or any other airport, became too painful relative to the fun of whatever destination was waiting for me.

Maybe I'm just a cynical old biddy. I know my great-grandkids use a different word. At least the ones who have anything worthwhile going on do. But like I said, I'm good with that. The only thing that worries me is boredom. The stuff going on in my head isn't quite so interesting to me any more. The frightening fact is that *nothing* seems all that interesting lately. Which was why I was particularly grumpy at my birthday party. I wasn't putting on a show so I could be alone with my thoughts. I was scared I was *done*. Done with people, done with thinking, done living. I supposed the fact that the idea scared me was a good sign, even if it made me ornery.

But life has a way of surprising you, even at my age. It was at my birthday party that something completely out of the blue happened to turn things around: I found a problem I could help someone solve.

The someone in this case was my granddaughter Jenny's husband, Will. He and I have a bit of history together. A number of years ago, he had the good sense to come to me with a problem, and I helped him get some perspective on it. Our conversations were great fun too, because I was able to play the grumpy old lady to maximum effect, and poor Will didn't have any choice but to put up with it because he needed my advice. I know I shouldn't enjoy that, but I've always been a big tease, and I think he'd agree we both got something out of the experience.

I hadn't seen a lot of Will since that time. I knew he'd been off flying around the country, trying to make things better at his company, and suffering the joy and pain that goes with that kind of job. I'd see him at family holidays and get-togethers, and occasionally we'd chat about various things work-related, but not in depth.

Which is why I was both surprised and pleased when he sidled up to me at the birthday party and said, "Can we talk?"

"Why, Willie, nice to see you, too," I said. He hates it when I call him Willie. "What's up?"

"It's a long story," he said.

"Willie," I said, "in case you haven't noticed, we're celebrating my 102nd birthday here. Time is not something I have much of. Can you make it quick?"

He got a pained look on his face. "I'll try. Remember about fifteen years ago, when I was coming to you with questions about change and project management?"

"Willie, I may be old, but I'm not senile yet," I chided. "Of course I remember that. Although it seems like you got less interested in talking to me once your problem was solved." His pained look worsened and I felt a little guilty pleasure at scoring a hit to his guilt center.

"You know how busy things can get," he said lamely. Then showed a bit of the fire that I like. "I don't have to bother you with more of that kind of thing if you're not interested..." His voice trailed off.

Too quickly I said, "No, no, that's all right. I can always listen. See if I have a few ideas." The bugger: I could tell by a slight movement at the corners of his mouth that he knew I wanted to hear about his problem. I didn't want him to start feeling comfortable, though, so I said, "Figured out that project management isn't the solution to everything, have you? Come up against some issues you don't think a dependency chart is going to solve?"

He sighed. "Well, yes and no. I mean, I always knew there are lots more tools out there. I've spent the last ten years or so learning about them and putting them into practice all over the place."

"Yes," I said. "You may recall we've talked about this once or twice." Like I said, Will and I had had a few chats over the years about management techniques and the latest management fads, but they never approached the intensity of our explorations around project management. I'd be lying if I said I wasn't more than a little disappointed that he hadn't come to talk to me more often.

"Yes, of course I remember," he said. "I always appreciate your insight into that kind of stuff." His voice trailed off as we took in the general mayhem around us. Great-grandchildren were laughing as they played with plastic toys and cell phones. Grandchildren, looking older to me than grandchildren have any right to, sat drinking coffee and catching up. My remaining children, wrinkled and bent, looked slightly bewildered by the scene, as people whose hearing, sight, and general mental acuity have started to diminish are wont to do. Why I was still around to see all of this, I had no idea. For a moment I craved my pipe more than anything. For several years now a single puff on the thing would send me into coughing spasms. There were still days when I thought the pain might be worth it, but to my descendants' relief, I'd given it up.

"Willie, let's take this conversation out to the porch. All these people are starting to irritate me." Slowly, I levered myself up and out of my chair, waving off Will's attempt to help.

"Will!" came the scolding voice of my eldest daughter, in whose house I now lived. "Give Mom a hand."

I couldn't let the opportunity pass. "Oh, shut up and leave him alone, Joanne. I don't need his help. And he doesn't need you nagging at him. I'm fine." Will and I walked slowly out of the living room. Everyone made a point of looking concerned. I'm sure some of them were hoping for a fall, a broken hip, and a quick decline. Nobody knows how much money I've got, and I'm not about to tell them, but I can see they suspect it's a lot.

The porch of my daughter's house is one of the main reasons I live with her. It's what people today might call a big, old-fashioned wraparound porch, but it's what I think of as normal. Houses today don't have porches, they have decks. And those decks don't look out over the street, where everything is going on. They're usually out back, looking over the neighbor's deck, which is full of people trying not to be obvious about looking right back at you. That's the way they build neighborhoods these days. Cramming more people into less space, and trying to create the illusion that we're not all sitting on top of each other.

Fortunately, Joanne's neighborhood has tree-lined streets full of big houses on big lots with big porches. These porches are places where a person can sit and think and watch the world go by. Or, in some cases, have real conversations with other people.

I lowered myself into the wicker rocking chair. Will sat down on the porch swing, looking uncomfortable. "Why don't you grab us a couple of beers, Willie, and loosen yourself up just a little?" That made him look even more uncomfortable, as I knew it would, but he disappeared into the house and came back a moment later with two bottles of cold beer. Giving up the pipe had been tough enough; I sure as hell wasn't about to give up the occasional beer. Of course, this stressed the relatives no end. Not that I really cared.

We sat in amiable silence for a minute or two, and then I said, "I ain't getting any younger." Will almost squirmed in his swing seat.

"It's a tough thing to describe, Martha, really tough. And it's mixed in with a huge sense of responsibility—"

"Jesus Christ, Willie, did ya hit someone with your car? Did ya knock Jenny up again? Steal food from the mouths of babes? What?" I love interrupting people with pithy comments like that.

Will ignored my digs. "It's work, Martha. It's got me in a funny spot, and I've never felt this kind of confusion about it before." I sipped my beer and waited, deciding against any more silly comments. The man actually seemed to be in physical pain. He got up and started to pace. "For the last ten years I've been the company improvement specialist. I go in and fix problems, make things better. Or at least, that's what I'm supposed to do. And I do more than just treat everything like a project. We've talked about that—all my training in those other disciplines and techniques. Granted some of them are more fad than substance, but there are still interesting ideas there."

"I remember, Willie." I wondered briefly if perhaps we would have talked more if I'd been a little less abrasive. But then where would the fun be in that?

He stopped pacing. "For the longest time, I believed I was making a difference, actually contributing something." He took a long pull on his beer. "But then things changed somehow. Or I changed. It was as if the rose-colored glasses had come off. I started seeing how, despite all the wonderful things I was putting in place, people pretty much kept doing what they had always done. We dressed stuff up, but once I left town and the project team rolled off, what was really different?"

I blew some air through my lips in an attempt to make a raspberry. Sadly, my lips were getting old, floppy, and dry, so it came out sounding more like paper rustling in the wind. "You're breaking my heart, Willie, you really are. Sounds like a good old-fashioned midlife crisis to me. Buy yourself a sports car. You'll be fine."

He gave me a look like a puppy that had just been kicked, which took the fun out of things. "It's like I don't understand people anymore. I thought I was pretty good at that sort of thing—understanding how people's minds work and using solid logic and rational thinking to help them. I had real success with that. But something feels different now."

It was my turn to sigh. "Youthful enthusiasm turning to middle-aged cynicism can do that to you," I said.

He slumped into his seat. "Martha, I don't understand why people do the crazy stuff they do. It doesn't make any sense to me!"

I belched loudly. Beer does that to me. Plus, I wanted to lighten things up a little. "I don't want to be contrary here, but it's not that complicated."

He looked at me skeptically. "Maybe not for you. Captain of industry and all that."

I shook my head. "We can get to that in a minute. But first, why don't you give me a few more specifics on your problem and why you're suddenly thinking about it now?"

My great-grandnephew Ethan chose that moment to come screaming onto the porch with Mr. Doodles, my rottweiler. "You be careful with him, Ethan," I said sternly. "Don't be too rough." Ethan is six and weighs forty pounds fully dressed and soaking wet.

Mr. Doodles, who was named by my daughter—I wanted to call him Spike—is 110 pounds of muscle and extremely good natured, so my concern was just for show. We watched them romp together on the front lawn.

Will kept his eyes on the two of them as he resumed. "I wanted to come back to Hyler to get off the road, but now I think this disconnected feeling was really at the heart of it. Traveling a lot wasn't so bad when I was loving what I was doing. I guess I thought if I came back here, everything would all fall into place again."

"Ah, my buddy Tommy, he said it best. 'You can't go home again.'"

Will looked confused. "Tommy? As in Thomas Wolfe? You knew him?"

I shrugged. "Don't change the subject." I love name-dropping. I got to know a surprising number of people for whom history has reserved space, though I like to keep Will guessing as to what's real and what's made up. It so happens that Thomas and I *did* spend a little time together in the thirties . . . but Will was talking again by then.

"Like I said, it all made sense. The company had a problem, I went there, we talked it through, I had a solution. All the people stuff just fell into place. I always thought the people part worked *because* the solution made sense."

"Willie," I interrupted, "if you tell me something made sense one more time, I'm going to have to hit you with this beer bottle."

"But that's the key part of the whole thing. I figured out the right approach, we did it, and it worked. The making sense piece is important, because now nothing seems to make sense, and it's driving me crazy!" He paused to empty his beer.

"Well," I said. "Maybe you could give me an example of what doesn't make sense, and we could use that as a starting point."

"Fine," he said. "The union at Hyler. Their actions make no sense."
"You've dealt with unions before, haven't you?"

"Well, a bit, but that's not the point. Right here and now, we have a crisis going on at Hyler. Our productivity sucks, the demand for the products we make is soft, and there is a real possibility that in the next year I'll be closing this place and moving all 500 jobs, 350 of which are union jobs, offshore. So you'd think the union would be at least somewhat interested in making things work, no?"

I wasn't sure if Will had any Italian heritage, but with the way he was waving his hands around, I was starting to worry for my safety. "I take it you're finding them less than cooperative?"

He shrugged. "That's one way to put it. We need concessions on wages, benefits, and pensions just to keep ourselves in the game, and we need serious concessions on the company's ability to schedule shifts, move people from shift to shift, and have unionized employees be able to take more ownership of the day-to-day supervision of the crews and themselves. We have so much supervisory and employee time tied up in figuring out how the collective agreement applies to the smallest activity, we can't get any work done. It's killing us! The shop stewards know it, the union rep knows it, the *employees* know it, but we're still stuck in this impasse, spending hours discussing grievances instead of producing stuff." His hands were waving furiously again, and he paused for breath with what could almost be described as a hysterical note.

"And as if that's not bad enough," he continued after a minute, "managing the nonunion staff is even worse. We have this complicated performance management system. For starters, it's based on a bunch of what we call 'competencies,' which are really just fuzzy descriptions of the skills and abilities people in different positions are supposed to be able to demonstrate. The real kicker is that every person gets rated on what is effectively a bell curve. That means that even if you have ten great employees, theoretically you can rate only one or two of them as great, most as average, and you're supposed to stick a couple of people at the bottom. It's having bizarre effects, where good people don't want to be on projects or teams together because it decreases their chances of getting a good rating. Whenever it's performance review time, people scramble to ingratiate themselves with their performance coaches so they don't end up on the wrong side of the bell curve. Before the review, there's horse trading among the managers; they move people around on the curve so it all fits. For employees, the process creates all kinds of suspicion, sabotage, and back-biting, and it encourages them to focus on the short term, not what's right over the long term for the company. Everyone knows that the system isn't working, but we sort of make it work by not following the rules completely, which makes it even more confusing. Still, good employees have been trickling out the door for the last three years. Based on everyone's assumption that I'm just here to close the place, I'm expecting it'll soon be a flood."

I clucked my tongue. "Ah, yes, sort of what used to get called stack ranking. Wonderful system for creating chaos and completely undermining the company."

Will grimaced. "Well, I'm glad you like it, 'cause it's certainly killing me."

I raised an eyebrow. "Surely Hyler isn't the only division that uses this at Mantec?"

He snorted. "We're not. I've run up against it several times, but the other situations were different; we weren't about to go over a cliff. I basically ignored the system and treated it like background noise, figuring that it would make my results a little worse, but that overall, things would improve. But after spending eight weeks back at Hyler,

I'm starting to wonder if this damn performance management system hasn't been causing a lot more problems than I realized."

"Interesting," I said, trying to look as if I was thinking about things. I wasn't really, at least not in any intense way. I'd seen many types of these programs back when I was still active in business. They all had a significant flaw no one really wanted to address. "But didn't you have to work within that system yourself?" I asked him.

"Funny thing is, no, I didn't. I was a special projects guy, reporting to Ralph. My teams formed and disbanded based on what I was working on. I never had a performance review, and neither did my teams. We were judged based on the short-term success of the project or the change we'd introduced. And because I had a way to manage that, it seemed to work out most of the time. Now that I think about it, though, we did lose some good people over the years in other places in the company. Never understood it then, but now..." He fell silent, watching the dog and little boy wrestle.

I thought it best to keep him focused, so I said, "Run along and get me another beer, Willie. While you're doing that, think about what else is causing you headaches at Hyler."

He disappeared into the house and returned in a couple of minutes with more beer and a bowl of corn chips. I made him go back for dip. When he was settled again, he said, "There's another performance management problem, though it didn't start that way. It's how we deal with our sales team."

I closed my eyes and interrupted. "Let me make a guess on this one. You have a good-sized sales group, and in these challenging economic times they've come under a lot of pressure around pricing. They've been discounting your products, most likely with the appropriate approvals, and it's helped sales. So much so that your volume isn't down all that much, but profit is way down, maybe even in the red. You talk to them about it, but you can't seem to change their behavior. Besides, it's better to be selling product and keeping people busy and the company in the marketplace than not. But you're losing money. Plus, a big part of your salespeople's compensation is based on commission, and the commission is calculated on the total sale, not its profitability. So while you're in the red as an operation, you're paying big bonuses to your salespeople. Like the old joke goes, you're planning to make it up on volume."

Will was shaking his head. "It took me a month to figure that out. No one has been looking at whether we're making money on an order-by-order basis. No one even knew how to do the basic calculation. When we figured it out, no one seemed to understand what it meant, and their biggest concern was that if we change the bonus program, the salespeople will quit. They don't seem to get that we're paying our sales crew to put us out of business!"

I laughed at that. "You know, Willie, I was kind of hoping you could come up with something new for me." I sighed, rather theatrically. "I guess I need to get used to being disappointed." I finished my beer.

He shook his head. "Yeah, yeah, you have a tough life. We young people are a big disappointment. We've all heard that story." He smiled at me like the Cheshire cat. Overall the effect was a little creepy. "But the good news is, since you've seen this all before, you've also solved it all."

This time there was no need to put theater into my sigh. "Well, the solution, if you want to call it that, isn't that complicated. But it sure as hell ain't easy."

FOUR

WILL GETS SOME PERSPECTIVE

MY CONVERSATION WITH Martha reminded me of an important life lesson: trying to wrap your head around a new idea can be downright painful. It requires you to think about something in a different way, from a different angle, and our brains aren't wired that way. What appears to have kept us alive for the last many millions of years is this: we figure out something that works, and then we keep doing it. We might have figured the thing out rationally, but more likely we came to it accidentally, or through trial and error. Whatever the case, our brain locks on that process or method, and from then on, all of our brain power is directed toward doing it over and over and over again, in exactly the same way. We resist change because the way we do the thing works, and we don't necessarily have time to screw around with something different. Our survival might depend on it. We fool around with a crazy new method for curing meat, the meat spoils, and the whole family starves the next winter. We try planting some new crop, it fails, and the family has nothing to eat the next winter. You get the picture. The whole "starving" downside is a powerful deterrent to making a change.

The problem is that this approach assumes our environment will stay the same; that we won't face new situations or new problems like, say, superbugs and global warming, or economic downturns and changes in consumer preferences. But hey, sometimes burnt orange is the new black, and that means black isn't cool anymore. Our environment is changing almost continuously, which means the moment we've worked out a way to solve a particular problem, the problem itself changes and our solution gradually works less and less well. But dammit, our brains don't want to keep reinventing the wheel; they want to mass-produce wheels! Our whole existence seems to be built on the idea that the path to wealth, happiness, and the American Dream lies in replicating the same thing over and over.

Sure, we talk about innovation, creativity, collaborative involvement, continuous improvement, and all those other things we're supposed to embrace. But when it comes right down to it, those things are a big pain in the ass. Who wants to spend all their time trying to come up with the next iPhone? Very few people do, and even fewer of those have the capability to do it. You're talking about a group of people that numbers in the thousands. With seven billion people and counting on the planet, statistically this is equivalent to zero people. Of that tiny group of highly innovative, creative people, some work at Apple, and the rest at companies you've never heard of. So what happens? Our systems, our processes, our people, and our products all get disconnected from the world. You're a Detroit car company making millions of cars that no one wants. It's been pretty clear for ages that you've been left behind. But you keep pumping out those crappy cars because... why? Because it's too hard to change what you're doing? Too hard to think about things differently?

A long time ago, Martha spelled out a few things for me that really struck home. What she said boiled down to a fairly simple set of ideas about change and improvement that apply in any context.

1. There can be no improvement without change.
2. You can't do it better unless you do it differently.
3. You can't do it differently unless you can *think* about it differently. This involves a bit of a leap of faith, but there's some thinking involved in trying to figure out a new way to do things. Which leads to:
4. You can't think about it differently without adopting a new mental framework, a new perspective, or, to use a word that can sometimes make people throw up a little in the back of their throats, a new paradigm.

Martha's point was that a mental framework is really just an organized collection of thoughts about how to deal with a certain situation. A framework is useful, because you get to figure something out once and then store those ideas in your brain for next time. We call the ideas a perspective or a paradigm. It's like having a little procedure manual in our heads that we follow every time the situation arises.

Of course, the problem with mental frameworks is that soon after we establish them, the world changes and our perspective needs to be revised. Having expended so much effort to get that new perspective, though, the last thing we want to do is revise it. Instead, we want to take it out into the world and use it to solve every problem we encounter. It's as if the natural industrial engineer in us wants to extract maximum value from every mental framework we develop.

The related challenge we face is thinking that once we have a solution, it will work on every problem. I fell into that trap for a while with project management. Once I understood the basic perspective on projects and familiarized myself with some of the tools that could be used, I tried to treat everything like a project. Turns out not everything *is* a project, though, and applying the project management process to anything that moved was not the best approach.

All of this was what I found myself coming back to with Hyler. I was searching for a perspective, a paradigm, that would help me deal with...what, exactly? When it came down to it, I was having trouble putting my arms around the problem. "I don't want to close the plant" wasn't a terribly helpful way to state the issue. Neither was "We're not as efficient as we need to be" or "Demand for our products is down," though all three of those statements were true.

When I took the opportunity to pull Martha aside at her birthday party and broach the subject of my struggles, she put on her regular sarcastic, crusty exterior, but I think it really made her day. I wasn't sure I should be pinning my hopes for a solution to the problems at Hyler on a woman who was turning 102 years old. But beggars can't be choosers, and Martha had once been a great source of ideas for me. In fact, as we got talking, I wondered why it had taken me so long to have another serious chat with her. After her regular number of digs and jabs, she had summed things up, as she always did, in a way that made me feel a little stupid.

"So, Willie," she said, "you've described a bunch of different issues, and you're telling me that things aren't good at Hyler. Would you say that's fair?" I nodded emphatically. "OK, well, that's fine, but I can't really help you with a bunch of random problems." She chuckled. "Actually, I probably could. But that doesn't seem to be why you're here. So what is it you want help with?"

I stammered, stuttered, and then went silent. Martha had a gift for making me feel like an idiot, and she was in full-on giving mode at that moment. To be fair, I probably deserved it. I had laid out a variety of complaints about everything from the union to the performance management system to how we paid our salespeople, but what was I really asking her?

I came up with a ploy to give myself time to think. I said, "Your beer is looking a little low, Martha. Can I get you another one?"

She snorted. "Take your time, Willie. And yes, I'll have another one, thank you, while you try to think this through." I got up and headed for the kitchen.

What was the problem I was trying to solve? What was wrong with the existing situation?

By the time I returned with two more bottles of beer in hand, I had made exactly zero progress on answering that question. When I admitted as much, Martha laughed and said, "It's not an easy question, my boy. But think on it a bit, and come back and see me when you're ready to talk some more." Then she smiled in a rather ghoulish way. "But don't wait too long, Willie. I might not be here."

THE FOLLOWING Monday I was in the Hyler main boardroom, staring at an empty whiteboard, trying to figure out how to answer Martha's question. I'd been sitting there since 6:15 a.m., hoping that an early start would lead to early insight and that by 8:00 a.m. I'd be heading to Starbucks to celebrate with a latte. It was now 9:10 a.m. and progress was negligible.

Misery being what it is, I decided I needed to share my struggle. Ten minutes later I had my senior team sitting around the table. Stu, Amanda, Leslie, Alice, Sheila, Mark, and Luigi stared at me in silence until Luigi ventured, "So this is it?"

"This is what?" I asked.

"The big announcement," Luigi said.

"Announcement?" I asked.

Stu sighed. "C'mon, Will, don't play games. The announcement about the plant closing. You called all of us in here with no notice on a Monday morning. What else could it be?"

Alice, as VP of accounting and finance, had the usual stack of papers in front of her. "Funny thing is, things have improved a little in the eight weeks since you've been back. But obviously not enough."

Amanda looked like she was going to cry. Mark Goldman actually had tears in his eyes. "It was a good run, Will," said Sheila.

I felt like yelling at all of them. Instead, I kept my voice as calm as I could. "Have you guys given up? You think things are that far gone? That I'd be back for only two months and then shut things down?"

Everyone looked at me blankly. Amanda said, "Is that a trick question?"

I looked up at the ceiling. "God help us!" I scanned around the room, looking into the faces of the members of my team. As I made eye contact with each one in turn, I didn't see a lot of hope in their faces. "No, this is not *that* meeting. The plant is not closing. At least not yet. We're here to have a very different discussion. One I hope is going to put that other discussion on permanent hold." If

I had been expecting a rousing cheer after my emotionally uplifting little speech, I would have been disappointed. All it earned was more blank stares.

"So you've got some ideas?" asked Stu. "Some new insight?"

"Not exactly," I told them. "In fact, exactly not. I feel as if I know less than when I got here."

"Nice, chief. Real inspirational." Luigi could be a sarcastic bastard at times.

"Not to be negative, Will, but you're looking at a group of people who have been busting their butts for three years now, trying to make this company work. Clearly we are out of ideas. Having us give it one more good old college try doesn't sound like the path to success." I preferred sarcasm to Alice's more rational truths.

"I'm not questioning anyone's commitment—" I started.

"—So you're saying we're incompetent," Amanda finished.

"—and I'm also not saying you're incompetent—" I continued, rolling with the detour.

Alice jumped in again. "Then you're not making me feel better. If we're not stupid, and we're trying hard, the only other conclusion is that this problem isn't solvable and we're all on the next boat to India."

"I think it would be Indonesia, Alice," said Stu. "India is getting too expensive."

"I hear Russia is the new spot for cheap outsourcing these days," Leslie piped up. "Then, in another five years, the U.S. may be so economically depressed that this will be the place to be and we can all come back home."

"Great," said Stu. "If we can just hold on long enough, we'll be the new developing world, and we won't have to move the operation anywhere. Maybe that gives us some kind of competitive advantage . . . we can stay where we are until the crashing economy makes us competitive again."

"People!" I interrupted, a little more shrilly than I'd intended. "At the moment, these are not things we care about. As I said, we're going to stay right here and solve our problems."

"Right, I forgot," said Amanda. "With the new ideas that none of us have. Yes, let's get back to that."

I stood up and began to pace back and forth in front of the conference room whiteboard. "Not that I want to dwell too much on the good old days, but some of you were around when we dealt with the Windsailor crisis. Remember that? We didn't know what we were doing then, and we managed to get through it."

"Well," said Amanda, "back to my point about ideas. Someone did have ideas then. You had that mystery consultant feeding us stuff."

"If it makes you feel better, I've been in touch with the same consultant," I said.

Suddenly, the mood in the room brightened. "Really?" said Amanda. "Why didn't you say that?"

I stopped pacing. "Oh, so now you're all enthusiastic? Like I wasn't bringing anything to the table? You need a consultant to get you motivated?"

Amanda rolled her eyes. "You already said you don't have any ideas, princess. And we've been coming up empty for a while now. So yes, some outside perspective is attractive. I'll try harder not to offend your delicate feelings in the future. But cutting to the chase, what has your guy got for us?"

I decided to put my ego aside, at least momentarily, for the good of the team. "She . . . uh, he," I started, and then had a furious conversation in my head about gender, honesty, and the value in correcting a little white lie.

When Martha helped us with the Windsailor situation, I was worried my team might not find an eighty-something-year-old lady a credible source of sound management advice. I portrayed her as a man, let the team paint their own mental picture of "him," and made sure the team never met her. I had never corrected their perception of Martha, and now I struggled momentarily with whether I should tell them the truth. Expediency won out: I had enough on my plate without facilitating a discussion about how my mystery consultant was my grandmother-in-law. So I carried on with the deception.

"He is suggesting that we need to go back to clearly defining our problem. He thinks we're spreading ourselves out in too many places, trying to address what are fundamentally symptoms of the same issue, not the cause."

Stu looked thoughtful for a moment and then said, "He's saying we're playing a game of whack-a-mole."

Mark Goldman, who had been silent to this point, upped his contribution significantly. "Huh?" he said.

Stu explained. "That goofy carnival game. My grandkids play it at the arcade. You plug in twenty-five cents—"

"Join the twenty-first century, Stu," said Alice. "It's, like, two bucks."

"—you plug in your money," Stu continued, "then you take this mallet, and mechanical moles start popping their heads up on the board in front of you. You try to whack as many on the head as you can before the time runs out."

"The difference is you get some satisfaction from that game. Here, there are always more moles to whack," Luigi lamented.

Mark must have had a late night, because it was taking him a while to get the concept. "So, in this case the moles are the problem?"

Amanda made a face. "Yes, Mark, the moles are the problem. You have a mole infestation in your house, or your barn, or wherever the stupid game is supposed to take place. You stand there like an idiot waiting for a mole to poke its head out so you can whack it. But you're not addressing the real problem. You're not going to get rid of the infestation by waiting for individual moles to appear and then whacking them. You've got to fumigate the whole house. Or nuke it, or whatever you do to get rid of moles."

"Nuke it?" said Mark. "Wouldn't that be a little extreme?"

"People!" I said. "As much as I love to wander off topic and relive my days working as a carny—"

"You worked as a carny?" said Amanda. "That explains some things."

"—which I just made up for effect! Can we get back to talking about the actual issue?"

"I think we are talking about it," said Stu. "We have a serious mole problem at Hyler."

"And instead of using nukes, we're dealing with the individual moles," added Amanda. "We're killing ourselves with the whacking, and we're not getting any further ahead."

"OK," I said grudgingly. "Maybe we are talking about the problem. But it's still an analogy, right? You're not going to tell me that our issues come down to an actual mole problem, are you?"

"Of course not. Don't be stupid," snapped Amanda.

Her comment was followed by an uncomfortable period of silence. Finally I said, "Analogies are great, but sometimes it's hard to understand what they are referring to."

Luigi commented, "It seems like an obvious concept, so why haven't we thought of this before?"

Mark had finally woken up a little. "That part I do get. We're so busy running around fighting fires that we don't have time to stop, take a breath, and consider whether we have a mole arsonist on our hands."

"So now the damn moles are lighting fires?" Stu sighed.

Mark shrugged. "You know what I mean. It's a common problem—going hard and not taking a moment to stop and think."

"I've got a story about that," said Luigi. "A guy is driving his car down a country road, and he passes a kid who is running as fast as he can, pushing a bicycle. The guy slows the car down, rolls down his window, and shouts to the kid, 'Hey, kid, what's the matter? What's the hurry?' Kid pants out, 'Late for school!' The man says, 'What's the matter with the bike? Got a flat?' The kid gasps back between breaths, 'Nope, bike's fine,' and keeps on running hard, pushing his bike. So the driver continues coasting alongside the kid and says, 'You don't know how to ride it?' Kid shakes his head. 'I can ride.' The driver frowns. 'So why are you pushing it?' Kid pants back, 'Told you, late for school. No time to stop and get on the bike. Gotta keep running to get to class!'" Luigi laughed long and hard. The best he got from the others in the room was a groan. "What, you don't get it?"

"Yeah, we get it," Leslie said impatiently. "The kid is so obsessed about making time that he doesn't realize if he slows down and loses a few moments to get on the bike, he'll get there faster. It's just that it's not remotely funny. And as parables go, I would rate it as weak."

Luigi shrugged. "Whatever. I can't help your poor taste in parables. But I think it shows what we're doing—running around solving little problems without taking the time out from firefighting to figure out the source of our mole arsonist bicycle problem."

"I think you can leave the bike out of that," said Amanda. "It's confusing enough as it is."

I decided to jump in. "That's exactly it. Unless we stop running around like chickens with our heads cut off and stop letting the moles start fires, we're never going to figure out...uh, if we have moles...or should I say, what the nature of our mole infestation really is."

Mark made me give serious consideration to whether he might be a mole himself by saying, "Why are we bringing chickens into this?"

I waved away his comment. "So, let's stop whacking moles for a minute. Let's stop even thinking about whacking moles, and let's answer the question: what is our mole infestation here at Hyler?"

"It's the union," said Luigi without hesitation. "And I can say that because I used to be a union member. They don't appreciate how bad things are. They just keep asking for more and more, and they're driving us into the ground."

"No," disagreed Amanda. "The union reacts to what we do to them. Our mole is corporate headquarters and all the crap they push down on us. Look at our so-called performance management system. It's totally dysfunctional and creates a totally dysfunctional workplace, including our crummy relationship with the union."

"Uh-uh," said Alice. "It's our sales team. Will, you're the one who pointed out they're discounting us out of business."

"Figures the accountant would say that," shot back Leslie. "My sales team does exactly what they're told to do. It's the accounting department that doesn't know what our costs are. How are we supposed to price things properly if you can't tell us that?"

Things were getting a little heated. Stu interjected in an attempt to be a calming influence. "Guys, it's all of those things together—it's us. The people in this room. *We're* the problem. And you know why? We're not on the same page."

Stu the calming influence didn't provide much calm. Everyone turned to stare at him. Amanda was the first to speak. "How can you possibly say that, Stu? I've been killing myself for the last four years trying to make this place work. And I'd say the same thing for every person in this room. You think any of us *want* Hyler to go under or offshore? You don't think we agree on that?"

Stu shook his head. "Having the same goal and acting like we do can be two different things. We all know our relationship with the union sucks, and we know we have to fix it, but what are we doing to make that happen? We just keep grinding on them, trying to make them give us more and more concessions."

"And all they do is push back on us," interrupted Luigi. "They just want to take. They won't work with us."

Stu cocked an eyebrow. "Are you saying that the union wants to close the plant? That they want the company to move all those jobs offshore?"

Luigi hesitated. "Well, no, I suppose not."

Alice jumped in. "The union doesn't understand how bad things are. They don't believe it when we tell them. They think we're bluffing."

Stu snorted. "Going from three shifts a day to two? Laying off half the workforce in the last few years? Seeing our production fall? Do you really believe they think we're just kidding?"

A light was starting to go on for me, though admittedly it was a bit dim. "Stu, you're saying that we and the union both want the same thing, or at least we want to avoid the same thing, but people aren't acting that way?"

Stu shrugged. "I'm not saying I can explain it, but think about it. We seem to be trapped in a pattern that's taking us down the wrong road, even though no one wants to go there. And I don't mean just with the union. I mean with everything from our sales program to our management systems to how we deal with safety.

We run around whacking moles, not seeing that we're actually whacking each other in the process."

"That reminds me of a story," said Luigi.

Everyone groaned. "Please tell me there are no moles or bicycles involved," begged Alice.

Luigi smiled. "No, but there are more animals. I'm serious, this is a good one." Luigi clapped his hands together and rubbed them, like he was warming up to perform a delicate operation or defuse a bomb. Or perhaps just to bomb. "There's this little frog: he's sitting by the side of a river, minding his own business. Suddenly a scorpion appears on the riverbank and comes crawling down toward the frog. The frog isn't worried, because scorpions don't eat frogs, but he's a little cautious. He knows the scorpion has a deadly stinger on its tail. So Froggy does a little hop right to the edge of the river and gets ready to go for a swim in case the scorpion starts to get crazy.

"But the scorpion calls out, 'Hey, Frog, wait! I'm not looking to sting you. I need a favor.' The frog is puzzled. 'Whaddaya mean?' he asks. 'What kind of favor?' The scorpion scuttles closer. 'A ride,' says the scorpion. 'My mother's sick, and she lives across the river. I can't swim. I need you to give me a ride on your back over to the other side.'"

"Wait a minute," said Alice. "If the scorpion can't swim, how could he end up on the opposite side of the river from his mother?" I was surprised it had taken this long for someone from the team to interrupt Luigi.

Alice continued to impress with her insights. "Maybe the story takes place in springtime, and the river is flooding. The scorpion moved out the previous summer, when the riverbed was dry." I started to wonder whether my *team* was the real problem.

Luigi was undeterred, having spent much of the last ten years dealing with these people. "Whatever. Let's not worry about that, because it doesn't really matter to our story, OK? So the scorpion asks the frog for a ride across the river. The frog shakes his head. 'Uh-uh,' he says. 'I'm not letting you get on my back. What's to stop you from stinging me?'

"The scorpion says, 'Look, Frog, I have no reason to sting you. I don't eat frogs. Plus, just think about it. I can't swim. We're half-way across the river, I sting you, what happens? We both die. Of course I'm not going to sting you.' The frog sees the logic in this and agrees to take the scorpion on his back."

"I can see where this is going," said Amanda.

Luigi ignored her. "So the scorpion jumps on the frog's back, and the frog starts swimming across the river. They get halfway across, and all of a sudden the frog feels a sharp pain in his back. 'What the hell?' says the frog. 'You stung me! Now we're both going to die! Why would you do that?' The scorpion shrugs—" Luigi held up his hand. "And before you tell me that scorpions don't have shoulders, I mean that figuratively. The scorpion shrugs and says, 'I can't help it. It's my nature.'"

I broke the silence after a moment. "I hate to admit it, but there's something about that story that rings true."

Amanda was nodding. "I hate to admit it even more than you do, Will, but I agree. Even though it makes no sense, even though the end result is bad for both of them, the scorpion still goes ahead and does it."

Leslie added, "It's also important that even though the frog knows it's a bad idea to carry the scorpion, he listens to logic and does it. And then dies."

Sheila spoke up. "So, what? We're not supposed to do any favors for anyone? Being nice gets you killed? What? I don't get it."

"Or," I said, "is the lesson that you can't change someone's nature? That scorpions sting, it's what they do, and there's no point in pretending any different?" I paused. "I don't see how that can be the moral of the story. We deal with difficult situations all the time. Nothing is truly hopeless. There are always ways around it."

"Yeah," said Mark, "but maybe the story means you can't take the obvious path. We're saying that we're the frog and the union is the scorpion, and they're stinging us even though they know they're sinking the company."

Stu frowned. "To be fair, I don't think you can say we're the frog. I think the union guys would say we're the scorpion."

Everyone started to talk at once, which confirmed for me that both mole whacking and the frog and scorpion saga were striking a nerve. As the babble continued, I went to the whiteboard and wrote down two things:

1. What is our mole infestation?
2. What does the scorpion's nature have to do with all of this?

I tapped the board to get everyone's attention.

"Here's where we are, people, and I have to say, we've made some progress." I pointed to the first question. "We know we have to take a step back, stop whacking at moles. Otherwise more will just keep popping up, and we'll get nowhere. We have to figure out what our mole problem represents, and then we have to find a solution that wipes out the moles entirely. Or at least one that leads to a major die-off." I tapped the second item. "At the same time, we have to figure out the scorpion's nature. I know Luigi told the story relative to the union, but my guess is it applies across all the major issues we've identified. Our salespeople, our internal performance management system—they are also examples of the scorpion stinging the frog, even though it's clear to both parties that stinging will sink them both."

At that moment, Hal Wilson, one of the shop floor supervisors, burst into the conference room. "We've got a serious problem," he said, breathing heavily from his dash down the hall.

"Don't kill us with suspense," Stu said. "What is it?"

"Strike," said Hal. "Well, sort of. The guys on the shop floor just walked out."

FIVE

WILL CONSULTS WITH THE FAMILY

I SAT IN THE living room, staring moodily at the fire. It isn't a gas fireplace, it's a real wood burner, and sometimes I imagine that wastefully consuming our diminishing wood supply in a ball of flame helps me to think. That's how my daughter looks at it, anyway. Which explained the discussion I found myself having instead of doing the thinking I was hoping to do.

"Seriously, Dad," Sarah was saying. "How can you burn up old-growth forest like that? It's not like that fireplace is even efficient at producing heat. Not to mention the greenhouse gases you're creating."

I hate to admit it, but my kids can really push my buttons if I'm not careful. "Honey," I said in a level tone, "this is not old-growth forest, and you know it. It's from our trees out back. An old-growth log wouldn't even fit in this fireplace."

Sarah rolled her eyes. Truly, one of the most annoying things in the world is the teenage eye roll. "Whatever, Dad. It's not going to have a chance to become old-growth now, is it? Fireplaces like ours are wasteful. It's bad enough that you work at that nasty factory, polluting the world. Why do you have to burn wood on top of it?"

"Sarah," I began, much more sharply than I'd intended, "that nasty factory is what allows us to spend the money that supports your environmental habit. It's what allowed you to go off to build houses in Costa Rica last summer, and it's what's going to pay for you to go to college next year, now that you're spending more time on the environment than on studying and won't be getting any scholarships!" That last bit came out more as yelling than the light conversational tone I was going for.

Sarah stood up. "Jeez, Dad, tense much?" She stormed out of the room as only someone infused with teen drama can do.

Jenny passed her as she came into the room. "A little quality father-daughter time?" she asked as she sat down. "Sounds like it went well."

I shook my head. "Beautifully. I believe getting angry at your kids instead of having adult conversations with them helps prepare them for the real world."

Jenny pursed her lips. "You do seem a little more tense than normal, honey."

I shrugged. "Maybe it's the fate of five hundred workers resting on my shoulders. Fifty of whom decided to take a four-hour vacation today to make their feelings about management clear."

"Uh-huh," she said. "And perhaps a little overly dramatic. I can see where our daughter gets it from."

"What?" I spluttered in protest. "Are you kidding me? I don't have a dramatic bone in my body!" Jenny just looked at me, which was far more infuriating than anything she could have said. I got up and angrily stirred the fire. "OK. Maybe I'm a little tense, but I really do feel as if the future of the plant is in my hands and I'm not making anything happen." It sounded like a good title for a depressing book: *Special Techniques in Not Making Anything Happen*. I was an expert.

"Is it the walkout?" Jenny asked.

I scowled. "No, that's just a blip. It was just a few guys grandstanding. I got them back to work the same afternoon, once I promised to listen to their concerns. But it's a sign of things to come."

"So why don't you go see Martha?"

I made a huffing sound. "For your information, I already did."

Jenny pretended to be shocked, making a big O with her mouth. "You've been seeing my grandmother behind my back? Again? Is it helping?"

I shook my head. "I really don't know yet. I'm scheduled for round two tomorrow."

"What was round one about?" Jenny asked.

I sighed. "I'm not 100 percent sure. She mostly made me see that I don't really know what the problem is."

Jenny smiled. "I can imagine she also told you it's hard to solve a problem if you don't know what the problem is."

"Ah, how well you know the old bird. I didn't need special coaching to tell me that, but it's funny how her perspective makes you look at things differently. I took her idea and went back to the team, and we made some progress. I think. At least I have something to report to Martha."

Jenny raised an eyebrow. "Care to share it?"

I shifted uncomfortably in my chair. "I'm not sure it's ready for prime time yet, honey." The truth was, I was uncomfortable talking moles and scorpions to Jenny without the background. It sounded, well, a little silly outside of the team discussion.

Jenny didn't buy it. "If you're not comfortable telling me, Martha is going to eat you alive. Why the hesitation?"

I was still reluctant, but I decided she was probably right. A dry run wouldn't hurt. "OK, fine. It's hard to tell you what came out of the discussion mostly because I don't fully understand it myself." The truth was, I didn't understand much of anything at that juncture, but I didn't want her to worry. "We had this long conversation that ended with two conclusions that are actually more like questions. The first question is, what is our mole infestation?" Jenny looked at me blankly. "And the second one is, what does the scorpion's nature have to do with all of this?"

"Wasn't that a Chuck Norris movie?" Jenny asked.

"Ha, ha," I said. "Let me give you a little context."

I proceeded to give her a brief summary of how we'd ended up talking scorpions and moles. When I was done, she looked thoughtful. "The mole part makes a lot of sense. I mean, how often do we spend our time treating symptoms without attacking the underlying problem? Our entire medical system is based on that idea." Uh-oh, I thought, don't get her started. Too late. "You know what the number-one-selling over-the-counter drug is? Heartburn medication. Because people would rather eat crap that puts their digestive systems in knots and then take a pill that gives them temporary relief than face up to the fact that they need to change their eating habits!" I could feel a bit of heartburn coming on myself. My wife has some very strong opinions on the medical system. She works as a freelance writer and lately has been doing a lot of work related to the issues with our medical system. "So I get the mole thing. You guys have heartburn, and you're trying different brands of antacids, hoping that one of them will work, when really, you've got to stop eating chili dogs with extra hot sauce."

"Exactly," I said. "Although that's where it starts to get fuzzier for me, and not just because you changed analogies. Although I have to admit that the chili dog is more appealing than moles—"

"That's not all," Jenny interrupted. She looked excited, which I assumed meant she was going to start in on the medical system again. I was wrong. "The scorpion problem. That's, like, the secret to the universe or something!"

I looked at her sideways. "Drama queen much?"

She shook her head dismissively. "Don't try to talk like a fifteen-year-old girl, honey. It's not a look that works for you. I mean, I run into the scorpion problem just about every day."

What I wanted to say was, "I seriously doubt you run into the kind of problem that is sinking a $500 million manufacturing concern that employs several hundred people and is causing your husband to secretly buy over-the-counter antacids every day." But I realized that might be taken the wrong way and interpreted as condescending and dismissive, resulting in me taking up residence on the sofa in the basement until I saw the error of my ways. I decided to see the error of my ways in advance and said, "Seriously?"

"Yes," she continued enthusiastically. "You're in a situation where it seems obvious what everyone should be doing, but people do exactly the wrong thing, the thing that makes the situation worse instead of better. And usually worse for themselves."

This wasn't making sense to me. "I'm not picking up what you're putting down, honey."

Jenny looked at me as if I was a little slow. Which, generally speaking, is the right way to look at me. "The simplest example? The kids."

I continued to draw a blank. "The kids," I repeated back.

"Yes," said Jenny. "We have two of them. Jake and Sarah. You may have noticed them around here occasionally."

"Ha. But what do the kids have to do with the scorpion problem?"

Jenny looked a little exasperated. "Sometimes I feel like we're from different planets when it comes to parenting!" I always get nervous when she starts down this line of discussion because we generally conclude that I have to change something I don't fully understand. "Haven't you ever noticed how sometimes we set clear expectations for the kids about something, including both the glorious rewards that will be theirs if they do what we ask and the horrible punishment that will follow should they fail to live up to the agreement, and then they go and do exactly what will get them punished?"

I did see what she was talking about. "Like Sarah going to her friends' parties." Maybe it's a father-daughter paranoia thing, but that one drove me nuts. "We set her curfew time and tell her all she has to do if she's going to be late is call and tell us where she is, why she's late, and when she'll be home. But what does she do? She comes home late, no call, nothing." We were currently in a cycle with Sarah where it seemed she was perpetually grounded because she couldn't make a simple call on the cell phone we paid for for exactly that purpose, which just compounded my irritation.

"Bingo," Jenny said. "It makes no sense, right? She basically stings the frog every single time, which results in her not being able to go out for two weeks. And when the grounding is lifted, it's a rinse and repeat on the whole cycle."

I was warming to the subject. "Or Jake and his smart mouth." While the Sarah situation seemed to always have me in the middle, this one was a Jenny-and-Jake thing. It had to do with the way they wound each other up, and it always resulted in Jake getting punished. It would start with Jenny asking him to do something like clean his room or dry the dishes. Jake would make some smart comment, to which Jenny would reply with something like, "Don't be disrespectful!" Jake would roll his eyes. Then Jenny would say, "That's five bucks off your allowance!" which would be followed by Jake saying something in her face about that being unfair. Jenny would escalate to ten dollars and no electronic entertainment for the rest of the day, Jake would say something more, Jenny would yell at him to go to his room, Jake would stomp up the stairs, Jenny would call, "Don't slam your door or it's no electronic entertainment for the week!" and Jake would promptly slam his door. I'd had several conversations with Jake about it, asking him why he couldn't shut his mouth after the first infraction, but he didn't have any good reasons. "I don't know, Dad," he'd tell me. "I just can't. I don't think Mom's being fair, so I can't stop."

Jenny nodded. "That's exactly right. The kid doesn't seem to get that every time he does one more thing, he loses one more thing. It drives me insane!" I didn't add that it seemed like she couldn't help herself, either; despite the fact that her method clearly didn't work, Jenny would keep ratcheting things up, just like Jake. I suppose Jenny could have pointed out that my grounding practices were having no effect on Sarah's behavior, but I just kept right on with that.

"So you see what I'm saying, correct?" Jenny asked. "Your problems with the union, or your performance management system, or your salespeople—those aren't Hyler problems, they're *people* problems."

I must have looked pretty glum, because my wife came over and rubbed my shoulders. "But don't worry, honey. I know you'll be able to figure something out. You always do. Especially with Martha's help." I patted her hand but didn't say anything. I had no confidence yet that my highly geriatric grandmother-in-law combined with my barely double-digit IQ were up to solving this level of problem.

SIX

MARTHA WEIGHS IN ON ALIGNMENT

THERE'S REALLY NOTHING good about getting old, except when you think about the alternative. I wish I could say that was my own line, but I have to tip my pipe to George Bernard Shaw. Although I'd be willing to bet dollars to typewriters he didn't originate it either. He just had better publicity people than anyone else. Sort of how life goes, isn't it? As the academics say, it's all about who publishes first.

Getting old means a lot of things, not least of which is that you gain an appreciation for things young people don't appreciate. Youth is wasted on the young. Dammit, there's another good line someone else takes credit for. You would think that living past one hundred and still having most of your marbles would give you license to claim some of these good ideas for your own. Sadly, no such law exists.

For me, and I suspect for many people, the worst part about getting old has been the disengagement. The gradual pulling back from the daily business of humans and society. Quite frankly, I've become less and less interested in the everyday drama of human existence. It's not that I don't like people anymore—not exactly. It would be more accurate to say I've simply become tired of the petty and superficial things that seem to occupy the majority of their waking moments. At the same time, I've become increasingly engaged in sorting through my life, my experiences, my *memories*, trying to make sense of it all. Trying to derive meaning from what, most likely, has been a random set of events that only have significance because I try to force it on them. Sort of like lying on a hillside and looking for shapes in the passing clouds. And when I start thinking like that, I become fairly certain that dementia has taken hold.

But occasionally something comes along that reengages me, that reignites a faint spark of interest in human society and human existence. I find it thrilling when that happens. It makes me feel better about my efforts to sort through my own life, too, because it is in those situations that I feel my sorting translates to something I can pass on. Is there any more profound legacy in this world than an idea shared?

Not that I wanted to give Will the satisfaction of knowing that, for the second time, his problems were providing a spark for me.

"Scorpions? Moles? Are you sure you weren't meeting your team at the bar, Willie Boy? Or smoking some of that funny grass young people like to smoke?" I didn't feel it necessary to acquaint him with my own experiences with marijuana.

Will was sitting on the porch swing while I occupied my customary spot in my rocking chair. He grimaced. "I wish we could meet at the bar. That would be a lot more fun. But no, no artificial substances, beyond some Krispy Kreme doughnuts and coffee, were used in the creation of these crazy ideas." I kept my gaze steady and said nothing. Finally he spread his hands and shrugged. "What else do you want me to say? That's what we got. And it seemed to be useful at the time."

I nodded slowly. "Not to give you a swelled head, but you're heading down the right road, Willie." The surprise and relief in his face were satisfying. "Personally, I tend to think about these things with fewer references to little furry mammals and arachnids. But the concepts are similar."

I reached down to the side table and picked up my beer bottle. It was empty. I held it up and waggled it in front of Will. He tsked. "I'm not sure replacing smoking with drinking is trading up, Martha."

As soon as he was inside, I let go with the coughing fit I had been suppressing. Nothing makes the relatives contemplate cutting you off from your vices like hacking up a lung, and it was something that was happening far too frequently. When he returned with two more bottles, I quickly took a swig to ease my throat and then continued. "I'm going to talk about the simple problem first, and then we can talk about the hard one. So we start with the moles." I took another pull on my beer and tried to collect my thoughts around the slight buzz I was getting from the alcohol. I went with one word. "Alignment." I waited.

Will had clearly been expecting more. "You mean like the alignment of the wheels on your car? Or the alignment of a road, or what?" I smiled. He scowled. "And this is somehow better than moles?"

I nodded and rocked. "Organizations spend a lot of time and effort talking about strategy and tactics, short-term objectives and long-term goals. It's often a good discussion, but what happens when they leave the boardroom and go back to work?"

Will thought for a moment. "If they're like us, they go back to whacking moles."

I smiled again. "That's pretty much it. They go back to jumping on whatever fire burns brightest, without thinking about what's causing the fire or how putting it out affects the big picture." I contemplated the yard for a moment. "You know how I hate jargon and catchphrases and cute little summaries of complex issues?" Will nodded. "Even though I hate 'em, sometimes they're useful. One of the ones I like is the three C's of strategy. Ever heard of it?" Will shook his head. "Clarity, Choice, and Consistency. Like most of these goofy little slogans, it's more of a mnemonic than anything. In this case, it's reminding us that for any strategy to be useful, it's gotta be clear enough for everyone to understand it. Making a choice about a course of action means being clear on what you will *not* do as much as what you will, because when you make a choice you are closing the door on other options. Trying to do everything is a guaranteed path to failure, unless you are just expecting to be lucky." I paused for another sip. "And finally, consistency. That's about commitment, about sticking with what you want to do."

When I stopped to take a breath, Will spoke up. "Hang on. Aren't you getting into tactics there with consistency? Aren't you talking about actually doing things at that point?"

I waved my hand in what I hoped was a dismissive gesture. When you're old, you have to be careful; what you think looks cool and casual can look feeble and demented to younger folks. "Don't jump on the semantics just yet, Willie. We'll get there. For now, think of consistency as the guiding principle for the selection and oversight of your tactics, rather than the tactics themselves. Are you with me so far?" He nodded and took another swig of his beer. "So, the greatest strategy in the world, if it isn't expressed clearly, doesn't choose one direction to the exclusion of others, and isn't implemented consistently, is not, by my definition, a great strategy. Conversely, a bad strategy that meets the three C's can actually drive things a long way forward, although possibly in the wrong direction."

Will looked thoughtful. "I don't see anything new in there, but it's not a bad summary. And it definitely applies to us. Our strategy isn't really the problem. We know what we do and what markets we're after and all that stuff. Our problem is execution. If we can't make our stuff efficiently, we aren't going to be in business much longer, but we can't seem to get our act together to do it. Everyone seems to be doing their own personal version of the right thing, which conflicts with every other version of the right thing. If we were a football team, we'd all be trying to take the ball from each other so we could score, confident that we're the only ones who can do it. And pissed off at everyone else for not recognizing that."

I nodded. "Yes, and meanwhile the other team is running up the score against you, because they are actually playing like a team. I've seen it before, Willie Boy, and it's not a pretty sight. That's where the magic word comes in." I stopped talking and looked at him in what I thought was a sage and meaningful way.

"What magic word?" he asked. "'Please?'"

"Alignment, Willie, alignment. Weren't you listening? In order to be successful, you must have your organization in alignment. What do you think that means?" I stopped trying to look wise and glared at him.

"Well, I suppose it means that what people are doing on a day-to-day basis is aligned with the strategy. And with each other. As a team. Or something like that."

I nodded. "Once again, you can see this is nothing new. Whether you state it explicitly, or understand it intuitively, everybody knows this has to be the case. But does everybody act that way?"

He stayed silent for a moment until he realized I was waiting for him to answer. "Well, obviously, no, they don't. They talk about it, but they run around whacking whatever mole pops its head up until it's time to go home and watch sports on TV. Or whatever they do to help them forget how frustrated they are at work with not making any progress. I find drinking is a good option."

I held up my empty beer bottle. "Speaking of which..." I was seized by another coughing fit while he was gone but managed to get it under control before he returned with two more beers. I continued. "Getting an organization into alignment is a difficult thing. There are very few out there that are in alignment or that can stay that way once they achieve it."

Will shook his head. "I'm not going to disagree with you on that, Martha. But if that's the case, why don't more companies fail? If achieving alignment is such a rare thing, why are there so many hugely successful organizations?" He stood up and began to pace back and forth. "I've seen several companies in the Mantec world that aren't in alignment. Many of them are far worse off than Hyler. Some of them have such a dysfunctional management team I had a hard time being in the same room with them. But they're cranking out money right now while we're struggling at Hyler. And my team at Hyler isn't nearly as fu— ... as screwed up."

I felt like laughing at Will's reluctance to use profanity around me. He wasn't the only one. For some reason, when you're 102 years old people seem to think you've never heard a bad word in your life, like maybe swearing hadn't been invented in my day. "Doesn't seem fair, does it?" I said. "Have I ever told you about the Monkey

Theory of Management?" Will shook his head. I continued. "In my rather long career, I came to understand certain things about business, and one of them is the MTM."

"Huh?" he said.

"Pay attention, Willie! MTM—Monkey Theory of Management. Keep your mind on the conversation. Anyway, as I was saying, I came to understand the MTM, and more than once I lived it myself. It goes like this: Most successful businesses are started by someone who has a great idea, one that is unique in the marketplace and contributes to filling a significant need. Sometimes the idea itself is not unique, but the way the company is able to deliver on it is. Either way, the person gets out there in the marketplace and finds that their idea, or their delivery on the idea, is so good that the money just flows in. The person, or the team, doesn't actually need to be great at management. The business model is so great that a monkey could run it and still make money. And so that is exactly what happens. The original idea guy or the original team aren't needed, so they get pushed aside by the monkeys, who have other objectives. The monkeys take over, and the monkeys have no interest in good management. They just want to enrich themselves, or they have other games they want to play. And because the business is so successful, their game playing is well funded.

"But after a time, even the greatest idea or the best structure is not enough to make a business work, and things start to go downhill. It's the monkeys who are in charge at this point, and they don't have any good ideas, nor do they know anything about management or alignment or strategy. So the business starts to collapse. The monkeys often try all sorts of silliness on the way down, but of course it's no use. They're monkeys, after all, and they never did understand what made the business run. Eventually things get so bad the business goes under, or someone who does understand the business manages to get control, fires all the monkeys, and puts a new non-monkey in charge. That person may be able to build things back up, creating a team of non-monkeys who eventually make the business successful again. And then the cycle begins over." I stopped to take a sip of beer. And yes, to feel a little self-satisfaction. I am a big fan of my Monkey Theory of Management. I think it accounts for much of what is wrong with the world today.

Will was looking at me like I had just shot his dog. "That's the most depressing thing I've ever heard. On so many levels." He slumped back in the porch swing.

"Why?" I was puzzled. I always feel good when I talk about my MTM.

He said, "First, you're suggesting it's inevitable that anything of value in human society will end up with people who will destroy that value, rather than do something good with it."

I thought about it for a minute. "Yep, that's pretty much exactly what the MTM is saying. You don't agree?"

He frowned. "No. And it's depressing to even consider that it might be true." He got up and started pacing again. "Secondly, what am I to Mantec and to Hyler? Am I one of the monkeys who's sucking the value out of the company? After a while, all that Lean Six Sigma Total Quality Management crap sure started to sound like monkey business to me."

I drank more beer. "That's a question you always have to be asking yourself," I allowed. "But I'll tell you something—monkeys generally don't ask it."

Will sat back down. "I feel so much better. Really. You are a tower of motivation. I can't wait to get back to work."

"Not yet," I admonished. "We haven't finished talking about moles and scorpions. Hearing about the MTM was just a little bonus."

Will muttered, "I don't know if my heart can take any more."

I ignored that and continued. "Getting back to the idea of alignment. Or more importantly, *creating* alignment. How do you know if you're aligned?"

Will thought for a moment. "I suppose it happens when everyone understands the strategy the same way."

I shook my head. "Not necessarily."

"Huh?" Will said. "Surely everyone has to agree on what the strategy is."

"Yes," I told him. "That's certainly helpful, and in fact highly desirable. But since you can't see inside someone else's head, how are you going to know if they understand it the same way you do?"

Will looked puzzled again. "If they can explain it the same way?"

I nodded. "You're getting closer. Let me put it differently. There's a famous expression that goes 'Actions speak louder than words.' Setting aside for a moment that speaking is an action, what is that expression really saying?"

Will could see where I was going with this. "It means what we actually *do* is the real test of everything. And you're saying that what people do is the best indicator of what they are thinking."

I clapped my hands. "Bravo, Willie Boy! That's a very important concept when you're talking about creating alignment. People's behavior is the only indicator that matters. It's people's behavior that produces products and systems and ultimately everything we're trying to accomplish with a business. Or with anything in life, for that matter. So while we might care what people think—"

Will cut me off. "What we really care about is what they do. It's the behavior that we want; it's the behavior that we need."

"Exactly," I said. "The behavior is what we need, not the sentiment. And behavior has the advantage of also being something we can observe, and count, and measure, and give feedback on. Which leads us to the big question, and the one your scorpion story poses so well: what drives people to behave the way they do?"

I started coughing again, and this time Will was there to see it. Maybe that was a good thing, because by the time I was able to get myself stopped, I was riding in the back of an ambulance with an oxygen masked strapped to my face. There's nothing like a dramatic exit to put the exclamation mark on an important conversation.

SEVEN

WILL TALKS ALIGNMENT WITH THE TEAM

THERE'S NOTHING LIKE someone else's near-death experience to make your own problems seem less intense by comparison. And there's nothing like watching someone you're in the middle of conversing with have a near-death experience to ruin your day. It sounds selfish to say it, but it's true. Even after they had Martha stabilized and resting comfortably, and we'd all left the hospital, my heart rate couldn't have dropped below 150 until the following day. Martha having an episode of . . . well, extreme coughing (which led to the breathing problems) had left me exhausted and in no shape to be doing what I was doing. Which was getting yelled at.

"There's no way we're going back on the floor unless you fix it!" Bert Maclaughlin, one of the union shop stewards, had worked himself into a lather, despite the fact that there was very little to get lathered about. "It's not safe on that floor, and you know it. Guys are crashing forklifts all over the place, and there's no protection for the guys doing assembly and working at the machines."

I remembered walking out onto the shop floor with Stu when I first arrived back at Hyler. My first comment had been: "What the hell happened?" What could best be described as a forest of stunted trees had grown up around the manufacturing space.

Stu had been with me and said, "What do you mean? Sure, we've expanded the space, added some machines, but it's not that different since the last time you were here."

I had walked over to the nearest dwarf tree (well, really it looked more like a dwarf tree stump) and slapped it with my palm. "What the hell are these?"

Stu had frowned. "Oh, those?" Stu had said. "Whaddya mean? They're impact posts, of course."

Impact posts are a safety feature you see occasionally at manufacturing and warehousing sites. They're three-foot-high steel-and-concrete posts set into the floor, which can withstand a reasonably significant bump from a forklift moving stuff around the floor. They're placed in front of equipment, shelving, and other assets that don't do so well if they get run into by the forklift. I'd seen them before, scattered across the floor at spots that are at high risk for an accident. What I was looking at was something else entirely.

"Stu, there should be a handful in a space like this. What I'm looking at is a frickin' forest. Have they been breeding?"

I brought myself back to the present and tried to be conciliatory, at least briefly. "Bert, we've planted a large number of impact posts to protect the workers out there. The company has spent a pile of dough at your insistence, and it's never enough. No one will take responsibility for driving safely. You expect us to make it idiot-proof on the floor, which you damn well know is impossible. Until you guys are willing to accept some responsibility for driving safely, nothing's gonna change."

Bert snorted. "Typical management. You don't give a shit about the safety of my guys."

I felt my irritation turning to anger. "That is a ridiculous thing to say, and you know it. How does it benefit the company in any way if the guys are crashing into machines or operators? Meanwhile, this union action is halting production on three lines. When we're not manufacturing product, we aren't making money. And when we aren't making money, that's threatening your jobs and the jobs of everyone in this plant."

Bert sneered. "I don't like threats, Campbell. This is bullshit. This union is not going to let you put our people at risk to make Mantec even more money. If there *is* a problem with making money here, it's management's incompetence, not the workers'." Bert stood up. "Install the new impact posts where we want them, or things stay shut." He walked out of the conference room and slammed the door.

I looked at Luigi, Stu, and Sheila. "That went well."

Luigi shrugged. "It never changes. Anything we say that doesn't involve spending more on whatever lame-ass idea they have is threatening the safety of the workers."

Sheila said, "Victor Hernandez called me three times this morning already." Victor was Mantec's chief financial officer, a serious control freak and about as cheap as they come. He was a big fan of Indonesian manufacturing. "Apparently, he can't seem to reach you, Will. He wants you to know exactly how much money we're losing every day that production is down."

I nodded. "Hence my mysterious lack of accessibility. The guy is practically drooling over how much money he thinks we could save if we closed down Hyler. I'd prefer not to talk to him if possible."

Stu shook his head. "Not smart, Will, not smart. You know Victor is Ralph's right hand. He's filling Ralph full of thoughts that he shouldn't be thinking. Next thing you know, the moving crew is going to show up, and we'll be shut down."

"Ralph is many things, Stu, but I don't think he'll go back on his word. We've still got some time to turn things around." At least I hoped that would be the case. Still, Stu was right; avoiding talking to the boss's right-hand man was probably not a good strategy. I badly wanted to have something positive to tell Victor, though.

Stu, Luigi, and Shelia stood up. "Moles to whack, frogs to sting," Stu said. "Gotta run."

"Enjoy!" I called as they left. My interlude was brief.

The conference room door opened, and Leslie Frame walked in with Stanley Almatta. Stanley's title was sales manager, but he was best known for the first word in his title. Stanley was one of those rare guys who wears his salesmanship on his sleeve like the worst of the used-car-lot bunch, but with sufficient honesty and warmth that you can't help but like the guy. Except not so much today.

Before Leslie could say anything, Stanley started in on me, all semblance of salesmanship absent. "Will, why the hell are you messing around with the sales incentive program?"

I did what I often do when there's tension in the air and I don't know how to react: I didn't react. I simply took a sip of my coffee and waited. Stanley kept barreling on. "The sales team is the only thing keeping this place afloat, Will. If my guys weren't out there busting their butts to move product, Hyler would be done. You start playing with that and you're putting all of our jobs on the line."

Leslie finally jumped in. "Will, I explained to him about the pricing—"

Stanley cut her off. "It's not the sales team's fault that you can't keep production costs down. We're out there selling this stuff at the best prices we can get."

I shook my head. "Stanley, listen to me. The problem is that the prices you're getting for our products are below our production costs. Do you know what that means?"

He snorted. "Of course, Will. I'm not a complete dumbass. But like I said, how is that our fault?"

I considered snorting back but didn't think it would make the right statement. "No one said anything is your fault. But right now, our sales incentive program is paying your team to put us out of business."

"I know you head office guys can be disconnected from reality," he retorted. "But haven't you ever heard of maintaining market presence? We may be losing money, but we're also maintaining our market share, and, Will, you do not want to lose that. You think it's costing us money now? You try and get that market share back. That's where the real money gets spent."

I took another sip of coffee and tried to stay calm. "Stanley, what was your average salesperson's bonus in the last six months?" I asked.

He pretended to think about it for a second. "Oh, I'd guess about 20 or 25 percent of base."

I pulled a sheet from the file folder in front of me. "The average bonus has been 37 percent of base compensation for the last six months. Greg Sanders has been averaging 62 percent of base—"

Stanley chuckled. "Yeah, that Greg is a real firecracker."

"—and you personally have been at 32 percent. If you look at the six months before that, you get a similar picture. It was before my time, but do you recall how the bonus program was changed when the recession hit?"

Stanley clearly could. "Not really."

Leslie jumped in. "Remember? We changed the structure to give the sales team a higher base so they wouldn't take too much of a hit during the crash. And we gave you more flexibility to set your own pricing."

I picked up the thread. "We also took the cap off the upside, so there was no limit to the bonus you could earn."

"And clearly it's working," Stanley said. "Look at the numbers we've been able to put up, even though the market is still way down."

I sighed. "So now we're paying the sales team even more money to sell our products at a loss. We're getting it coming and going, aren't we?"

Stanley was back to looking angry. "So, once again, it's our fault that your production people can't keep costs under control?" He stood up. "Look, you do what you gotta do. All I'm saying is, we're the people who are keeping this place going. We're the ones keeping Hyler's products in the marketplace, and without us, this place is toast. You mess with this incentive program, you're putting the entire company at risk." He turned to Leslie. "I'm outta here before I say something I can't take back." He stalked out.

Leslie glanced at me, slightly embarrassed by her employee. "At least he didn't slam the door," she said weakly.

"Thank God for the little things," I said.

Leslie looked timid, which was not normal for her. "So, what do you want to do, Will? I mean, I get what your concern is about selling products below cost, but he does have some good points about market share..." She trailed off.

"What good is market share if we aren't in business? Are you telling me that Stanley earning $200,000 a year with the new sales incentive program, as opposed to $100,000 under the old one, has nothing to do with his stand on this?"

Leslie shook her head. "Will, Stanley is one of the longest-serving members of the sales team. He's been here for twelve years. I don't think he'd ever do anything to hurt the company. He knows his job is at risk. We all do."

I stood up and paced the room, hoping I was projecting the image of a caged jungle cat rather than the scared, middle-aged manager I was. "But if he's so loyal to the company, how can he keep pushing for something that is killing us?"

"I think—" Leslie started.

"Rhetorical question," I said. "That's our scorpion problem, and so far we don't know the answer."

Leslie cut to the chase. "So what do you want to do? Are you going to change it?"

I paced some more, batted some more things around with Leslie, and then did pretty much the worst thing I could have done: nothing.

TO BE FAIR to me, which I think is very important, I didn't actually do nothing. I had another six impact posts installed to placate Bert and the union. I was confident they added nothing to safety, but they matched the decor and got our production folks back on the job. And I got the team back together to talk about my conversation with Martha.

"And that," I concluded with what I hoped was a flourish, "is what alignment means, and it's clearly what we are lacking." I looked around the table at my team. Stu, Sheila, Amanda, Luigi, Leslie, Alice, and Mark gazed back at me. I had just finished explaining Martha's theory about alignment and mole whacking and was hoping to see a little more excitement on their faces.

Sheila spoke first. "What you're saying has merit, Will. We do have a relatively clear strategy, and there's no question we are lacking in the alignment department."

"But?" I prompted.

"But," continued Stu, "you're missing the punch line. You've reframed our discussion in better terms, and 'alignment' definitely sounds more professional than 'mole whacking,' but what it's really coming down to is the scorpion gambit."

"Pardon?" I asked.

Stu shrugged. "OK, so gambit isn't the right word. I was going for effect. But it's the scorpion issue that's at the heart of our problem now. We know we need to get across the river. The frogs and scorpions agree we need to get across the river. But right now we're in the middle of the damn river, and we're all stinging the frog. Or each other. Or both. 'Cause despite the fact that we all know where we need to get to, we aren't *acting* in alignment. What did your consultant have to say about that?"

Everyone looked at me expectantly. They were still under the slight misconception that my consultant was from some high-end strategy firm whose hourly fee was equivalent to the GDP of a small Central American country. I didn't think it would help their spirits to hear that our expert was in hospital with a lung fluid problem. "We didn't get to that part in detail." I told them. "We ran out of time."

I didn't bother to share Martha's Monkey Theory of Management. It didn't seem as if it would be all that helpful at this point.

"You ran out of time?" Sheila asked with a dramatic flourish, much better executed than my earlier attempt. "In case you haven't noticed, *we're* running out of time!"

I shrugged. "Look, she... he said we were on the right track with the scorpion thing, so long as we understood it in the context of alignment. He said that was the mechanism by which we could create alignment in actual behavior. And then he had to jump on a plane. But he said in the meantime we should think about why people do things. Which is what I want us to spend a few minutes on now."

Mark stirred restlessly in his chair, and Amanda looked at her watch a little too obviously. "Jeez, Will, I've got about a million things to do to keep the frogs from sinking in the river. Is now really the time for this?"

"Yeah," said Leslie. "I get the alignment thing all right, but people are people, right? They just do what they do."

Stu looked a little more interested. "No, that's not exactly true. I can tell you that Stanley, for example, doesn't do what he does for no reason. He does what he does because we pay him to."

"C'mon," said Mark. "Don't you think that's too simplistic? Are you saying that Stanley is only motivated by money? You don't think he cares about this place?"

Stu shook his head. "Not exactly. I'm sure he does care about Hyler. But I'm saying that right now our sales incentive program is paying Stanley and his crew to sting the frog. He knows it, we know it, but we're giving them money to do it. We're paying them to behave out of alignment."

Sheila looked genuinely puzzled. "Well, if he knows he's stinging the frog, and he knows he's going to drown, why is he still doing it?"

Stu smiled. "Because we're paying him to. I just told you that."

Leslie jumped in. "But if he really understood the implications of it—"

Stu cut her off. "Why is it we assume that if people could understand better they would stop doing what they're doing and do what we think is the 'right' thing? Anyway, I think Stanley understands perfectly well. But every day he comes to work, and we say, 'Do this thing and we'll reward you.' We want him to sell, we pay him for it, we promote him for it, and that's what he does. Leslie, what would you say to Stanley if he walked into your office tomorrow and told you he thinks the right thing is for him to sell less product, not more. Would you promote him? Give him a bonus?"

Leslie was caught off guard. An unintelligible mumbling sound was the best she could muster.

"Exactly," said Stu. "Or let's say Stanley takes it on his own initiative to keep his prices higher because he knows we're losing money. Suddenly he's making us money on each sale, but he's not selling nearly as much. What happens to his bonus?"

Sheila answered for Leslie. "It goes down. Not to mention that the other salespeople who aren't trying to do the 'right thing' are going to keep earning their big incentives."

Stu spread his arms. "Understanding the world has nothing to do with it."

Mark was having none of that. "Sorry, Stu, but I don't believe that's true. People aren't scorpions. They don't just do what feels good in the moment. They're complex organisms who weigh pros and cons and make choices. They may not always make the right choices, but the more they understand—"

Sheila interrupted. "Actually, Mark, I don't think that's true at all. In my experience, doing what feels good in the moment is *exactly* what people do."

Mark looked around the room. "Jeez, that is the most cynical thing I've heard yet today. Do the rest of you agree with that?"

Leslie was nodding. "Maybe not quite to that extent, but..."

"But what?" demanded Mark. "What do you see every day that would possibly make you buy that? Are we just rats in a maze, trained to run after the cheese someone has put out at the end?"

"I don't know," said Leslie, "but I watched my brother-in-law quit smoking about a hundred times. He knew it was bad for him. He had heart trouble. He saw his father, who was a heavy smoker, die of emphysema. His doctor told my brother-in-law he was killing himself, but he still kept smoking. When he was diagnosed with lung cancer, he decided it was too late to quit, and he smoked right up until the day he died. He knew cigarettes were killing him, but he kept on smoking them."

Mark looked disturbed by the story, but he wouldn't let go of his point. "That's different. Some people have addictive personalities. They can't help themselves."

Amanda chimed in. "So you're saying that the scorpion theory is as simple as 'people can't help themselves'? If that's the case, what do we do to prevent getting stung?"

"Well, if you believe that, you put up impact posts," said Luigi. "You try to set things up so that no matter how stupid or careless people are, they can't sting themselves." He shook his head. "But we know how well that works. Just when you think people can't get any dumber, they find a way to drain a little more intelligence out of the pool." He thought for a minute. "It's as if the guys on the floor are deliberately testing the boundaries to find a hole they can drive a forklift through to prove that the place isn't accident proof."

Mark looked increasingly agitated as Luigi spoke. "That's just not true, Luigi. People aren't like that."

Stu nodded his head. "I agree, Mark. That's not quite what happens. But just like with the sales crew, Luigi's guys are doing what they do because we pay them to do it." Mark made a grunt that sounded like a question. At least, Stu interpreted it that way. "I'm glad you asked. 'Cause it's pretty damn simple. We don't reward the guys on the floor for not having accidents."

"What are you talking about?" Mark asked. Even Luigi looked puzzled.

"I agree, that one is a little more complicated than with the sales force," Stu said. "But when you really drill in, it's very similar, only in reverse. With the sales people, we're paying them to do the wrong thing. With our people on the floor, we're *not* paying them to do the right thing. And we're also not giving them much in terms of consequences for doing the wrong thing. We simply try to idiot-proof things even further. I bet the average guy in the shop isn't even aware of the accident rate."

"That's not true," protested Mark. "We have a big sign that shows the number of days since the last lost-time accident."

Luigi said, "C'mon, Mark. That's a joke. The guys pay no attention to that. I think they have more fun when it gets reset to zero than anything."

Stu was nodding in agreement. "I've been around this place longer than any of you. I've seen us go from having a good safety record to having a bad one and back again. And I can tell you, we've created a culture of bad safety right now. And the union is part of it."

Mark was flapping his mouth like a goldfish that had jumped out of its tank. "You're getting crazier by the second. It's the union that does nothing but harp on safety all the time. They're the ones *driving* our safety programs."

Stu smiled. "And yet things continue to be bad. Or to get worse. Tell me, Mark, what's in it for the union if safety isn't a problem?"

Mark made an exasperated noise. "Don't be silly, Stu. What's in it for the union is that their members are safe. People aren't getting hurt. There's no production downtime. There's everything in it for them."

Stu got up and went to the whiteboard. "Interesting fact, Mark: we haven't had a guy hurt—"

"Or woman," chimed in Amanda.

"—or woman," Stu corrected, "hurt on the floor in more than two years." He wrote "no injuries" on the whiteboard.

"That's true," said Luigi. "No one has been hurt. But lost time due to accidents is way up."

"Exactly," said Stu. "So no one is hurt, but we're losing production at a significant rate, which is driving up our costs, which is part of what's driving us out of business. If we can have more accidents without anyone getting hurt, ask yourself who benefits."

Mark was getting visibly upset. "Seriously? What is this, some kind of conspiracy theory? Stu, nobody benefits from accidents. You're talking crazy."

I decided to weigh in. "That's not entirely true, Mark. What got Dale Richmond reelected as president of the union local?"

Amanda answered. "He made a big deal about safety. And even though he yaks on about it incessantly, the reality is that the accident rate has increased since Dale got back in."

I nodded. "It benefits Dale for accidents to be a problem."

Mark was incredulous. "So you're saying Dale is going out and sabotaging the place?"

I shook my head. "Not at all. I'm saying there's an upside for him in it. He benefits from having an issue with management." I turned to Luigi. "And tell me what happens when one of the shop floor workers backs into a machine or whacks the storage rack."

"We shut things down while we check for damage and maybe fix something."

"And what do the workers do while that is going on?"

He seemed to get where I was going. "They go outside and smoke cigarettes. Or go grab a coffee. Or play cards. But they don't work."

Stu jumped in. "That's what I'm getting at. I'm not saying this is all deliberate. I'm just saying, that in the moment, good things happen when there's a minor accident. People benefit, at least in the short term. And we're part of making that happen. We pay people to be in that situation. We reward them. We create the environment." Stu wrote "workers benefit" and "union benefits" and "Hyler creates the environment" on the whiteboard.

I walked over to the board and circled the last item. "Guys, we create the scorpion's nature. We reward or discourage or punish everything that goes on here. On the surface, it might seem weird to say anyone is better off for a lost-time accident, but the reality is, we don't make anyone better off for *not* having an accident. In the moment, there's even some incentive to have one. Management creates all of that."

Mark stood up. His face had gone completely red in the last few minutes. "I have another meeting, but even if I didn't, I wouldn't want to stay for this. What do you think we are, a bunch of pigeons pecking keys that light up because we get food when we do? Do you think people are stupid, or that they do the wrong thing because they're evil or something?"

I shrugged. "Mark, I don't know the answer to that. That's why we're talking about it. What I do know is that what we're doing at Hyler isn't working. That means we have to consider the possibility that our understanding of the underlying situation is wrong."

Mark was shaking his head as he walked out. "It's about respect for people. You guys are just looking for someone to blame."

There were a few minutes of uncomfortable silence after he closed the conference room door. Finally Amanda said, "Another successful meeting."

Leslie added, "I think Mark's really buying into this."

Sheila, who had hardly spoken, said, "What does it say when our HR guy is checking out of this approach?"

We all looked at each other. It seemed appropriate for me to say something bold, inspiring, and leader-like. Instead I just opted for what I was thinking. "We feel uncomfortable because he's saying things all of us are feeling. But it doesn't mean what we're feeling is right, or that the approach is wrong."

And with those inspirational words, and no real ideas about what exactly we could do to solve the problem, the meeting broke up.

"HONEY? HONEY?" The voice seemed to be coming from a million miles away. Well, that's a little exaggerated, because it's impossible that I would have heard it at all from that distance, not to mention the logistical challenges of getting a million miles from anywhere without there being outer space in between you, and of course sound doesn't travel in a vacuum...oh, boy. You can see why my wife was having trouble getting my attention.

"Mmmmm?" I mumbled, my mind returning reluctantly from space and merging back into my body, which was sitting in our living room with Jenny.

"Tough day at work?" Jenny asked. "Lots to think about? Should I be doing a house-hunting trip to Kuala Lumpur?"

Along with being a fountain of useless trivia, I am fairly good with my geography. "Kuala Lumpur is in Malaysia, honey. We'll be outsourcing to Indonesia, so you might want to think about Jakarta for the trip. Although we'll most likely be out in the country-side, where manufacturing space is cheaper."

Jenny raised an eyebrow. "You know what I mean. What's with the thousand-yard stare and the deafness?"

"What?" I said.

"What's with the...oh, very funny. What are you thinking about?" she said, with a little edge to her voice.

"It's the scorpion problem. We still haven't solved it, and it seems to be the key to avoiding having to get used to a much higher level of humidity for the rest of our days. Also volcanic eruptions and occasional military violence."

Jenny nodded sympathetically but didn't say anything more. I decided to try out an idea I'd been mulling over. "Remember our conversation a few weeks ago about Sarah and her curfew?"

Jenny and I had a few simple rules with regard to our kids being out in the evening. The first rule: Mom and Dad need to know where you are. That meant telling us before departing the house, and then updating us if plans changed. The second rule was that unless there was permission given to change it, curfew time had to be respected. Showing up past curfew, without having cleared the late arrival with a parent, was an automatic grounding: two weeks of no time away from home except for school.

The third rule was that calling *before* curfew time, providing rules one and two were respected, could sometimes lead to a nego- tiated change in the time they needed to be home. Jenny and I thought these rules were fair, and they put responsibility on the kids, with clear consequences for breaking them. We needed to know where the kids were and that they were safe. As long as that was the case and it wasn't a school night, missing a few hours of sleep to stay out late was no big deal.

Jake had no trouble with this arrangement, and he frequently negotiated a revised curfew time. Sarah was a completely differ- ent story. For reasons we couldn't understand, she was hugely resentful that she had to let us know what her plans were. By various means (usually the parents of her friends), we could always determine that she wasn't up to anything particularly wor- risome, but she had spent most of the previous year being grounded because she didn't want to tell us where she was going or call us when she was going to be late. As far as we could tell, hanging out with her friends was the most important thing in the world to her, and yet she acted in a way that prevented her from being able to do it.

The situation drove us nuts, me especially. As you can imagine, Sarah was not the happiest person to have around the house during her frequent groundings, and unhappy teenagers have a surprising ability to make everyone around them unhappy.

Jenny was shaking her head. She made a noise that sounded like "Aaaarrrggh!" and then switched to English. "I've been trying hard to forget the last year, but I think it will be burned into my brain forever. It has been my most unpleasant year as a parent. So far, anyway. I live in terror that she'll be here forever."

"Wait, what?" I said. "I mean, who?"

"That unhappy, demented girl who has taken the place of our daughter for the last year that seems like a decade."

"But why does she do it?" I said. "Why does Sarah do the very things that prevent her from getting what she most wants?"

Jenny thought for a minute. "It's pretty simple, really. What we think is the most important thing to her really isn't."

"I'm not quite following," I said.

"Well," Jenny continued, "we have our objective, which is keeping our kids safe. We've been assuming that Sarah's objective is to maximize the amount of time she can hang out with her friends. That seems important to her, right? Following our rules should really be a minor inconvenience for her to get what she wants."

"It really *is* a minor inconvenience!" I said. I could feel my heart rate going up as I thought about how frustrating it was that Sarah couldn't follow a few simple rules. And how irritated I felt at always having to be the bad guy.

Jenny interrupted my heart-attack in the making. "But hang on, Will. That's what I'm saying. Maybe her friends aren't the most important thing. Maybe it's something else."

"Like what?" I asked crankily, thinking Jenny must be off her rocker.

"Like her independence. Or at least her interpretation of what that means. Maybe it's more important for her to exert her independence from us than it is to hang out with her friends."

I wasn't buying it. "You're saying she would rather be yelled at and grounded than make a simple phone call and be able to hang out with her friends?"

Jenny nodded. "That's exactly what I'm saying. She's a teenager, right? And you know how much she has resented our rules, right from the start. Remember all her arguing, with her saying we didn't trust her?"

I winced. "Yes, I seem to have a vague recollection of that."

"What she really wants is to feel independent. To *not* have to check in with Mummy and Daddy. That's the most important thing to her. She still wants to hang out with friends, I'm sure. But our assumption about what's really driving her—maybe we've been wrong."

I was feeling an awkward combination of confused and enlightened. "So, if we go back to the scorpion story, you'd be suggesting that the reason the scorpion stings the frog, even though he knows it means they're both going to drown, is that he gets so much immediate pleasure from the stinging that the drowning isn't really on his radar."

"Yes, I guess something like that," Jenny agreed. "Her desire to be independent, or to act that way, means that Sarah is continually stinging the frog—which is to say, not calling us—and then drowning—which is to say, getting grounded—even though that seems irrational to us." She stood up. "But then, what the hell do I know? What does anyone know about teenagers? I'm going to bed. Reliving all the drama of the last year is making me tired."

"Wait," I said. "This is making some weird kind of sense to me, but there's kind of an important question we haven't answered. How do we make it stop? How can we get her to start calling and letting us know where she is? How can we get her to stop stinging the frog?"

Jenny was drifting toward the hallway. "I wish I knew. 'Cause that would really increase my chances of surviving the teenage years."

EIGHT

MARTHA IS HOME WITH MORE ADVICE

I WAS HAPPIER and more emotional than I expected when I finally found myself back in my rocking chair on the front porch of my daughter's house, watching the wind rustle the leaves in the trees, smelling the air, and generally not being in the hospital. Near as I can tell, the purpose of a hospital is to provide the illusion of doing something constructive for an old person while you're waiting for them to die. I suppose the purpose could also be to infect the old person with some nasty bug in order to speed up the process. Regardless, I was damn happy to be home again.

That lasted for a day or so, and then I realized I was missing something: Will. Maybe not Will exactly, but I was certainly missing his problems. At least the ones he wanted my help in solving. Luckily, I didn't have to wait long for us to get back into it.

"Great-gramma!" The tone wasn't all that enthusiastic, but I could understand why that might be the case. Sarah is fifteen, and to her I'm sure I look like an Egyptian mummy risen from the dead. She gave me a halfhearted hug—maybe she thought I'd break if she squeezed me—and then headed for the basement rec room.

"Gramma!" This, from my granddaughter Jenny, was much more genuine, though her hug also conveyed the impression that I was made of glass. "You're looking good! They must feed people well in the hospital these days."

I smiled. "You're full of shit, honey, but thank you for saying it."

I got what I believe was "Higramma" followed by some grunting from Jake, who followed his sister to the basement, and then Will stood shifting awkwardly from one foot to the other in front of me. Being related by marriage, and also being a little intimidated by me, Will has never been sure just what is appropriate in terms of displays of physical affection toward me. I've never bothered to clarify, because it's more fun that way.

"Hello, Will," I said. "Back to make me choke some more?" He laughed uncomfortably but didn't say anything.

"Oh, Mom!" my daughter Joanne admonished me. To Will she said, "She couldn't wait for you to get here, Will. Whatever you two were talking about, she wants more. Just try not to let her get too excited."

But of course there was the usual family conversation about how all the great-grandkids were doing in school, and whether the president was doing the right things for the economy, so it was a good hour before Will and I were left alone. We weren't quite alone, either. Jenny stayed sitting there with us.

"Will has been telling me about the scorpion and the frog, Gramma," she said. "I know he's thinking about the story because of work, but it seems to me it applies more broadly than that, so if you don't mind, I want to listen in. It might help me with the kids."

I smiled at her. "With kids, sometimes nothing helps, but you're welcome to join us." I gave her a crusty smile, but her long face remained. "I'm joking, Jenny. Joking. Human behavior is human behavior and it works in a very consistent fashion. Even with teenagers." I paused for a moment. "Especially with teenagers."

I stared meaningfully at the two of them until finally Will said, "What?"

I nodded toward the kitchen. "There's something I need to get me going here."

Jenny shook her head. "Oh no, Gramma, the doctor said the carbonation in the beer was likely what caused your coughing fit. You're not supposed to be drinking any more of it."

I sat up straighter. "At this stage in my life, immediate gratification is the same thing as planning for my long-term health. I don't much care what the doctor says. Willie, can you do the honors?"

Will jumped up and went in the house.

"He hates it when you call him Willie," Jenny told me.

"I know," I said. "That's why I do it." Jenny laughed.

Will returned with two bottles of beer and a glass of red wine for Jenny. I took a sip of beer and tried to make myself comfortable in my rocking chair.

"So, where were we?" I asked Will. Not that I needed any help remembering.

Will did a little recap. "We talked about alignment, and why that's important. But we didn't get to why people don't do what makes sense, even when the alignment is clear. You were going to explain to me why the scorpion stings the frog, even though that means he drowns."

"What I'm wondering," Jenny interrupted, "is why Sarah won't follow our simple rules and instead keeps doing exactly what she knows will get her grounded."

I smiled. "Ah, yes, the secrets of human nature. The mystery with all the clues hiding in plain sight." They both gave me a puzzled look. "The information I'm about to impart to you is well known to everyone. In fact, it's the basis for how we interact with our environment, and it's the basis for the functioning of human society. We all know it intuitively, at a fundamental level. But we don't like to think of ourselves as functioning in this manner, so we ignore it a lot of the time. As a result, we create endless problems for ourselves.

"Don't get me wrong. This isn't the solution to everything. It's not some magic potion that cures all of the world's ills in an instant. But understanding the underlying structure of why humans behave the way they do and having a language and framework that allow you to talk about it makes it possible to solve some problems that you might think are intractable." I smiled with pleasure. When you're my age, finding a way to work a fifty-cent word like "intractable" into a conversation doesn't happen every day.

I looked at my audience of two and gestured expansively with my beer bottle. It's hard to make a decent expansive gesture with a beer bottle, and I don't recommend you try it at home. "You guys ready to see what's behind the curtain?"

Will smirked. "Yes, O Great and Powerful Oz. We've got to get Jake to a baseball game in a couple of hours, though, so please don't start with the big bang unless it's absolutely crucial to our understanding."

"I'm glad you youngsters get the reference. I've got a story about meeting Judy Garland on the set of that movie—" I held up my hand. "Don't worry, we won't go there. But for this trick I will need a pencil and paper." Will must have been planning to take notes himself, because he had a pad with a pen all ready to go. "Right then. Let's get started."

NINE

WILL SHARES THE PERFORMANCE PRINCIPLE MODEL WITH THE TEAM

THEY SAY IF YOU truly want to understand something, you should try teaching it to someone else. I've had that experience a few times in my life. I was reluctantly setting myself up to have it again now as I shuffled nervously from one foot to the other in the conference room.

In attendance was my senior management team: Stu, Amanda, Leslie, Alice, Sheila, Mark, and Luigi. Sitting in the center of the table was a box of something comprising many parts sugar, some parts flour, and a whole batch of chemicals, commonly known as doughnuts. A fine mist of icing sugar swirled lazily in the air. A tumbleweed blew across the boardroom table...but only in my mind. In reality, people were shifting impatiently in their chairs.

"Is this going to take long?" asked Alice. "I've got a crapload of month-end stuff I gotta get to."

"I appreciate the sugar fix, as always," said Luigi, "but I've got lots to do to hold up my end of running this place into the ground." No one laughed.

"Yeah," said Stu, "so dish. What's the big breakthrough?"

"Well," I stammered, "I don't think I used the term 'breakthrough'—"

"Whatever," continued Stu. "You said you had something to tell us about understanding the scorpion's nature. So let's have it."

I cleared my throat. These days everything seemed to make me nervous. I've given speeches at conventions in front of a thousand people without thinking twice about it, and here I was sweating about having a general conversation with a few coworkers I'd known for fifteen years.

"OK," I began, "fair enough. Just to recap, we agree we're clear with our strategy at Hyler, but we've been stubbing our toes on understanding the mechanism that gets everybody aligned with our tactics. As we've taken to referring to it, we've been struggling to understand the scorpion's nature. Why is it that our different teams don't act as if they're aligned, even though they should be?"

"Yeah," said Stu. "Although you might want to phrase it more like 'Why the hell do people do the stupid things they do when the right thing is so obvious?'"

"You're a cynical bastard, ya know that?" Leslie said. She didn't look like she disagreed with him, though.

"Ah, yes," I continued, pretending there had been no interruption from Leslie. "Something like that, Stu." It had all been obvious when Martha walked me through it. I was hoping I could translate that to my explanation. "In order to tackle this problem, we need to take a step back and define our framework for this discussion."

"That sounds like consultant-speak to me," Sheila said.

"Yeah," I countered. "But you guys all know this consultant. Sh—, uh, he hasn't steered us wrong yet. Am I right? You know how obsessed he is with language and communication. He lays stuff out this way so we can get a handle on it." At least I hope I have a handle on it, I thought to myself. "Shall I continue?" When no one spoke, I repeated, "We need to step back so we can home in on the problem we're trying to solve."

Mark piped up. "I thought we were trying to solve the scorpion problem. You know, the psychology of what the scorpion is thinking, what's going on inside his head that makes him do the wrong thing."

"Exactly," said Alice. "What childhood bed-wetting trauma made the scorpion the nutjob he is today."

"Such that he'd rather sting the frog and drown than not sting at all," added Amanda.

"To sting or not to sting," Mark offered.

"Whether 'tis nobler—" began Leslie, but I shut her down.

"All righty then," I said. "I'm happy you're such a well-read crowd, but let's focus on the first important element of our framework. What do we know about the scorpion?" The answers came back rapid-fire:

"He's nuts."

"He's a killer."

"He's stupid."

"He was beaten as a child."

"He feels guilty about all the frogs he's murdered."

"He has a death wish."

"Erectile dysfunction."

"He's repressing something."

"He actually knows how to swim, and he's just pretending he can't so he can kill another frog."

I jotted some of these on the flip chart as people rattled them off, then pointed at the list. "Really? Do we really know these things about the scorpion?"

"We know there's something wrong inside his head," said Mark. "If there wasn't, he wouldn't be stinging the frog and killing himself."

I nodded. "Fair point, at least from our perspective. But what's the problem with trying to understand what's going on inside someone else's head?"

Everyone thought about that for a minute. Finally Mark spoke up again. "Will, that's what your consultant is supposed to have the answer to."

"Isn't that what all your Myers–Briggs personality profiling is supposed to do?" Alice said to Mark. "Isn't that why we have to answer all those questions about what vegetable we would be if we were a vegetable?"

"Complete garbage," Stu said, with emphasis on the "garbage" portion of the sentence. "I don't know what you HR guys think we get out of that, but it's a total waste of time."

"Hang on," Mark said, clearly offended by Stu's comment. "That 'garbage' is extremely helpful in explaining things like people's communication and learning styles. It helps team members to function more effectively together."

Stu shook his head. "I don't care if one of my team members is a feeling introvert who likes long walks on the beach and fruity drinks with umbrellas. That doesn't help me when I'm trying to work with the guy." He nodded at Alice and Amanda. "Or girl. Lady. Woman.

Whatever. Knowing Mr. Scorpion's learning style doesn't mean anything when he's sitting on my back with his stinger out."

"Maybe his stinging is part of his communication style," countered Mark. "Once we understand that, we can factor it into how we deal with him."

"Oh, good God, Mark," said Stu. "Surely you're not suggesting that therapy sessions for the frog and the scorpion are going to help?"

Mark answered with as much defiance as he could muster. "Absolutely. Although maybe 'therapy' is the wrong word. What the hell else are we going to do except try to understand him?"

Stu was on a roll. "I don't want to understand the bastard! I just want him not to sting me in the back when I'm taking him across the river! Understanding is not at the top of my list at a time like that!"

"Maybe it should be," said Mark huffily.

I thought it was time to step in before they came to blows. "I like the way you guys are going," I said, "despite the threat of violence in the air. Because this is where we need to change our thinking a little. Let me ask you a question, Mark: how can we observe someone's thoughts?"

He stared at me for a minute. "Huh? Literally, of course, you can't."

I smiled. "Exactly. We can't. We have no way of knowing what's shaking inside someone else's head. Is that a problem?"

Alice answered. "I think we can agree it's a huge problem. Otherwise, we wouldn't be sitting here waiting for Stu and Mark to go all MMA on each other." There was a mixture of head nodding and eye rolling, except from me, since it took me a few seconds to get the reference to mixed martial arts. My kids would have cringed.

"Good!" I said. "As we continue to find, agreeing on the problem is an excellent starting point. So we can't see inside someone else's head. Barring some crazy technological breakthroughs, we will never be able to."

Amanda looked impatient. "So what are you saying, Will? There's no way to solve the scorpion problem?"

I shook my head. "Not exactly. I'm saying there's no point trying to solve it by expecting there's a magical way to discern someone's thoughts. Looking for a solution that relies on that as its starting point is not going to help us. But there's something we can see and measure that is actually more important than whatever craziness is swirling around in all of our heads. Anybody want to guess what it is?"

People looked blank. The silence stretched out, and I started to lose my nerve. I was about to tell them when Stu saved me. "It's what people do." There were a few questioning noises from around the table. "It's what people do," Stu repeated. "Whatever messed-up stuff people might be thinking, none of it matters, because in the end they do something. We can see that, measure that. And in any case, that's what we're trying to influence. It's not what they think, it's what they do."

"Exactly!" I said, hoping I sounded enthusiastic and not simply relieved. "It's what people *do* that really matters. And like Stu says, we're trying to produce a bunch of people who do the right things, regardless of what they're thinking."

Amanda frowned. "But what you think controls what you do. How can we ignore what people think?"

Mark wasn't comfortable with the notion either. "Yeah, that's dumb. What if some production scheduler thinks six plus seven equals eleven and so doesn't schedule the right components on the right machines and the whole final product delivery schedule is thrown off?"

Stu jumped in again. He was really getting the hang of this. "You can't manage what you can't measure. I can't measure a production scheduler's mental arithmetic directly. All I can measure is the result of it. And I can't measure what the scorpion is thinking. But I can see him sting the frog."

Now I actually *was* getting excited. "And therein lies our challenge. We're used to thinking that what goes on inside people's heads is what's important. And it is. It's just that we have no way of actually seeing that. What we do have is an *indicator* of what's going on inside someone's head, and that's their behavior. And it's like Stu says: what people actually *do* is what we're trying to manage anyway." I paused to take a drink of water and let my words sink in. "We can see behavior, we can measure behavior, and ultimately we can *manage* behavior."

Mark, it was obvious, was far from convinced. "You can't ignore what people are thinking. Thinking is what makes us human. You can't just pretend that our heads are some kind of black box."

I nodded as vigorously as I could. "That's exactly what I'm saying, Mark. Well, maybe not quite. What I'm saying is that since we can't see inside other people's heads, the most practical and useful thing we can focus on is what they do. Who here has seen a person say one thing and do another?" There were some hesitant grunts and half-raised hands.

Leslie seemed clear on the concept, but she was puzzling out the implications. "I think I get what you're saying, Will. I even agree with what you're saying. But here's my question: so what? It's more practical to focus on whether the scorpion stings or doesn't. It doesn't matter what he says. Or thinks. Great. But how does that help us?"

I went up to the whiteboard and wrote:

"I'm getting to that, folks, but this is our starting point. Let's say that 'B' right there represents the behavior we want. That's our target, our holy grail, our nirvana—"

"Let's not go too far, Will," said Alice.

"Right," I said. "But it's a big shift. Our focus changes from worrying about what a person is *thinking* to what a person is actually *doing*."

Alice was still skeptical. "I'm not sure that's such an earth-shattering change, Will, but whatever."

"Just stay with me," I said. "And it will all make sense." I hoped. "It's what a person does that counts. We can see their behavior, right?" I continued. "But why do we actually care about what they do?" I was greeted by no response, so I added, "What happens when the scorpion stings the frog?"

"They both drown," said Amanda, rather cheerfully I thought. I hoped she wasn't imagining the same fate for me.

"Excellent," I said. "And what happens if the scorpion doesn't sting the frog?"

Amanda hesitated for a moment as if she suspected a trick question. "Uh, they both don't drown?"

"Precisely!" I said. "And when it comes right down to it, what is it we're trying to achieve in this situation?"

Stu answered this time. "Presumably, we're trying to achieve 'not drowning.'"

"Bingo!" I said. "We're trying to achieve 'not drowning.' I know that may sound a bit uninspiring—"

"Yeah," said Luigi. "It's a bit like achieving 'not failing.'"

"It's an example, team. Stay with me." I went to the whiteboard and added another letter:

I turned back to the group. "Remember how a second ago we said we didn't really care what people were thinking, we cared what they were doing? Well, I'm going to take that a step further. Practically speaking, we only care what people are doing because what they're doing affects the result we're trying to achieve. In other words, we care about behavior because it's behavior that will give us the result we want. We want people to engage in the behavior that will give us the result we need. That's why I drew the 'B' with an arrow to the 'R.' The behavior drives the result."

"I love frogs and scorpions and all," chimed in Leslie, "but can you relate this back to something more tangible?"

I nodded. "Sure. I don't want to get too complicated too quickly, but let's talk real world here. What's one of our biggest concerns on the shop floor these days?"

A chorus of voices replied, "Safety!"

"Right. So 'safety' is the general result we want to achieve. We have to define that result more carefully to make it practical. As we've been discussing, we do have lots of measures of safety, like number of lost-time accidents, or—"

"Or the number of idiots who drive their forklifts into production equipment!" said Luigi. "I could do with a whole lot less of that."

"Great," I said. "Good example. All those impact posts that have sprung up. Why did we build those?"

"So that idiot forklift drivers who aren't paying attention ram the friggin' impact posts instead of the equipment," Luigi said vehemently.

"Exactly," I continued. "So we're concerned not just with the safety of our people, but about the safety of the equipment. And how has that strategy of building impact posts worked for us?"

It was Luigi who answered again. "You know already. Accidents have gone up. It's harder now to maneuver out there on the floor, and the guys pay less attention than they used to because they know the posts will protect them. It's like we've taken all responsibility for good driving away."

"Right," I said. "By trying to idiot-proof the shop floor, we lowered the common denominator for idiot. Let's relate this back to the model on the board. The result we wanted to achieve was fewer crashes. But instead of addressing the behavior that was causing the problem, we put up impact posts. Essentially we said, 'You can keep on driving the way you have been; we'll just make it so you can't crash into the machines.' So we didn't really solve the problem, did we?"

Alice looked a little excited. "We just created another mole to whack!"

Amanda looked less excited. "Great—love those bad analogies. I'd almost forgotten about the mole-whacking one."

Alice continued undaunted. "But it works in this case. We try to solve a problem, but we don't get at the root cause, and so we end up transferring the problem somewhere else. Now, instead of spending time repairing damage to production equipment, we're fixing forklifts that get damaged from hitting impact posts, and we're treating whiplash and losing time because the guys on the floor are still hurting themselves." She thought for a minute. "It's like, for the frog and scorpion, we decided to solve the problem by having the frog wear a Kevlar bodysuit so that the scorpion couldn't sting him. But then halfway across the river, the Kevlar is too heavy for the frog to swim in, and they still both drown."

"I hadn't thought of it that way," I said, "but you're right. Instead of looking at the behavior that will get you the result you want, you try to solve the problem another way and create more problems." I looked around the room. "So, when we're trying to problem-solve, why is it that we don't we address the problem behavior?"

No one said anything for a minute. Finally Sheila ventured, "Because we don't know why people do the things they do? Like you said, we can't see what goes on in people's heads."

I turned back to the whiteboard. "Ah, but here's the thing: we actually *do* know what drives people's behavior. Consequences!" I added to my diagram:

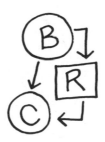

No one said anything, which I took as an invitation to continue. "You know that saying 'For every action, there is a reaction'?" It was actually a shortened version of Newton's third law of motion, rather than just a saying, but I thought Sir Isaac would be OK with me doing a little editing. "Well, for everything we do, there's a consequence. For example, you're six years old, you walk up to a hot stove. You reach out your fingers and touch the burner. What's the consequence?"

"Fried fingers?" said Luigi.

"You have to clean the burner," offered Amanda.

"You feel pain," said Stu.

"I'm going to go with door number three," I said. "You feel pain. The consequence of your behavior, touching the stove, is pain. And what impact does that consequence have on your behavior?"

"You don't touch the stove next time." Stu held up his right hand and showed us the palm, where a scar was visible. "It wasn't a stove, it was a campfire. And it wasn't a burner that was glowing all red and pretty. It was some coals in the fire that were begging to be picked up. Oh, and I was four, not six."

"Ouch. Very nice personal drama to help make the point. Thank you, Stu," I said. "The result of that consequence, as Stu says, is that you don't touch the stove, or the glowing coals, the next time. I'm going to show that on our diagram, like this." I drew:

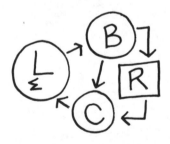

"'C' is for consequence, of course, and that 'L' with the little sigma symbol underneath it represents a person's learning history.

It's the sum of all the hot stoves you've touched, all the ice cream cones you've licked, all the tests you've cheated on, all the dogs that have bitten you. Basically, that's the accumulation of all of your experiences, including behavior and its consequences, in the black box that is your brain, guiding you toward your next scorpion bite. Or away from it."

Amanda said, "So, you're saying it's our learning history that determines our behavior?"

I nodded. "Yes, and one more thing." I added another symbol to the diagram, so that it looked like this:

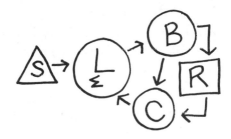

I pointed to the symbol I'd added. "The 'S' in the little triangle stands for 'stimulus.' Anyone care to guess what that means?"

"If it's where the U.S. government steps in and gives Hyler a pile of money, then I'm all for it," suggested Stu.

I laughed. "No, not quite. The stimulus is anything that creates an occasion for a particular behavior to occur. Really, 'situation' might be a better word, except that it's too passive. The stimulus is the thing that gets put out there to prompt the behavior."

"Such as?" Stu said. "There's a prompt for you."

I laughed again. "Everyone's a comedian. Let me turn it around and ask you, Stu. What was the stimulus for you touching the coals?"

Stu didn't hesitate. "Just seeing them. I still remember how they looked."

Leslie spoke up. "How does that help us, though? I mean, if some guy driving a forklift sees a piece of production equipment, that's his stimulus to ram it? Do we put blinders on him or something?"

I shook my head. "No. Well, yes. Sort of. You need to figure out the occasion that prompts or stimulates the behavior. In some cases, you might be trying to change the stimulus. In others, you need to learn what prompts the behavior. It depends on the situation."

I decided to start at the beginning of the process and work forward. "Let's walk through the whole model, and see if that puts everything in better focus. It all starts with the big 'S'—stimulus. A person is walking along, happy and carefree, when suddenly there is a stimulus. Let's say it's four-year-old Stu, and he sees the glowing coal in the campfire. The colored object is his stimulus. What happens then?"

The crowd looked uninspired, so I continued. "The stimulus gets processed through his learning history. What did your learning history tell you the first time around, Stu?"

Stu grimaced. "Nothing about the coal being hot."

I nodded. "Exactly. In fact, you probably got some brain feedback about touching cool-looking things being fun. We'll never really know, nor does it matter, because what happens next is important. The behavior. The thing we can observe and measure. Little Stewie touches the glowing coal."

Amanda said, "His head does remind me a bit of that weird little kid on *Family Guy*."

I ignored the chuckles around the table and continued. "So then we have two things. First, there's the consequence to our subject, and we already talked about that. Little Stewie feels pain. But what's the result?"

Stu said, "In my case, it was camping trip over and a ride to the hospital, and some serious verbal pain for my dad when my mom heard about him letting their darling child mess around in the fire. Not to mention scars and a strong desire not to burn myself again."

"Right," I said. "The result is what happens externally, which is, or contributes to, the end objective we're trying to achieve. Or in this case, avoid. There's one more key thing that goes on here. What is that?"

Stu continued to be my poster child. "My learning history got updated."

"Exactly. Which meant that the next time that stimulus occurred, you behaved differently." I paused. "You did behave differently next time, didn't you?"

"Of course," said Stu. "Unlike my lifelong relationship with tequila, I didn't need to repeat that behavior multiple times."

I smiled. "One thing that's important to note: we have no way of knowing exactly what goes on with someone's learning history. Quite frankly, the person probably doesn't either. And it really doesn't matter. We put it in the model almost as a placeholder to represent the idea that something inside of us is keeping track of behaviors and consequences, and is constantly updating the information."

I sat back down at the conference room table and pawed through the empty box of doughnuts, looking for crumbs.

"I don't know," said Amanda. "I mean, I get how you're saying all of this works. I don't exactly disagree with it, but it seems a little..."

"Simplistic," said Leslie. "Or else really complicated, if you think about, say, trying to analyze my sales team's behavior and results related to the selling process."

My internal voice was telling me she was right. But my Martha voice was telling me to shut up and believe in what my consultant had told me. I didn't have a chance to see which voice would come out of my mouth, because at that point Jill Eastman, one of the executive assistants, knocked on the conference room door and then walked in without waiting for a response.

"Will, it's Ralph on the line, and he says it's urgent."

Everyone looked at me. I knew they were all thinking the same thing: our time had run out.

TEN

A NEW WRINKLE: WILL ADDS MORE DETAIL TO THE MODEL

"SO THAT'S IT? Hyler's done?"

Jenny looked as if she was going to cry. I felt a stab of guilt for drawing out my account of the day to extract maximum drama.

"No, honey, no. I'm sorry. I was just trying to make the story a little more dramatic."

Relief washed over Jenny's face. "So what's the rest of the story then?"

I discovered that I had a glass of Scotch in my hand and I took a sip before answering. Alcoholic beverages had become more regular companions of late. "Ralph started off all gloom and doom, railing on about how it's been almost four months and I haven't turned the place around, time to shut the operation and move to Asia, yada yada. The regular spiel."

"Surely he realizes that four months isn't enough time to sort everything out. I thought you guys talked about a one-year time frame?" Jenny said.

"Oh, we did. But Ralph's point is that things don't turn around on day 364. There's a trend of improvement that indicates when things are moving in the right direction. He's seeing no trending yet."

Now Jenny looked a little pissed. "That's not true. What about all the process improvements you've been making? You've shown me some of the stats—production is up slightly, the union situation has settled down, things *are* getting better."

"Technically you're correct, honey. Some improvements have been made. But according to Ralph, it's not enough, and not enough is falling to the bottom line."

"So what's he saying?" Jenny asked grimly.

I drank more Scotch. "That we have to make more dramatic improvements, and we have to have them within four more months."

"So he's cutting your time frame almost in half? And what does 'more dramatic' mean?"

"It means we need to be profitable for a month four months from now, and we have to be able to demonstrate we'll sustain profitability going forward."

Jenny frowned. "What was the last profitable month Hyler had?"

I pretended I had to think about it, but I knew the answer. "The last time Hyler made money was almost two years ago."

My poor wife was horrified. "That long? Why didn't you tell me this when you took the job? How can you turn around two years in the next four months? No wonder Ralph wants to close the place down."

I shrugged. "I told you things were bad."

We sat in silence. I finished my Scotch and poured myself another one.

"What about Martha?" Jenny asked. "Is what the two of you talked about helping?"

I nodded. "Well, yes. But it's taking me longer to get my head around things than I thought. And I've got to try and get my management team on board with it. We were actually just in the middle of a session when Ralph called."

"Where'd you get to?"

I brought Jenny up to speed on where I'd taken things, and how people on the team were reacting to the ideas. "We've still got to have the whole punishment and reinforcement discussion, but I want to let the earlier material sink in before I get to that."

Jenny shook her head. "I don't think you have that kind of time, honey. I'd say it's education overdrive time. You guys will still have to figure out how to actually do something with this stuff."

"Yeah, I know. I just wish I had some real-world experience with this approach."

"Will, honey, that's the wrong way to think about it. Remember what Martha said? This is how people interact with the world. Period. It's not some new thing you're trying to impose. It's simply an explanation for why things happen the way they do. If you accept what she's saying, and I don't know that you have much choice at this point, you have a lifetime of experience to draw on. We all do. You may not have experience in a work environment at adjusting the circumstances in a conscious way to change the outcomes. Although we've all done that, too, even if we didn't realize it at the time." Jenny came and sat down beside me on the couch and put her arms around me. "Honey, you've got to get back at it with the team in the morning."

THAT EXPLAINS WHY the very next day the cat came back...well, the team came back, anyway. I called another emergency meeting to do two things.

They sat around the conference table looking irritated, frustrated, and annoyed that I was wasting more of their time in meetings when they should be working. The Krispy Kreme doughnut centerpiece had done nothing to improve the mood.

"First," I said, "the news from head office."

"We're done, aren't we?" demanded Leslie.

"No, not quite," I answered. "But we have a slightly shortened time frame in which to make things happen."

"Shortened," asked Stu, "or impossible? It's an important difference."

"Shortened," I said firmly. "It'll be challenging, but I think it's doable. We've got to show a profit, for the month, within four months."

After the exclamations of disbelief, anger, and general grumpiness, I continued. "I realize how that fits with what's been going on, but it's better than the alternative."

"Which is?" asked Mark.

"That we close down now," I told them. No point in trying to soften what Ralph had said. "The practice of offshoring has become a big part of Mantec's strategy, but it's not some kind of political statement; it's about what makes business sense. And our CEO is about nothing if not that. Ralph doesn't want to close Hyler down because he doesn't like us. He wants to close us down because we're losing money, and we've been doing that consistently for close to two years. He actually thinks highly of the team here, and his point is that if a group like this can't make the place run, nobody can. Eventually, he's got to stop letting us try. He told me initially we'd have a full year, and my conversation with him yesterday doesn't really change that. It's just that we need to show we're moving in the right direction sooner rather than later. You all know we've made strides in the last few months."

Stu's face was glum. "Yeah, we've made some improvements. But they've been incremental changes. We need a quantum shift to make this place truly work. How do we get a quantum change in four months?"

I pointed at the whiteboard and the drawing from yesterday. "Right there." Everybody looked again at my handiwork.

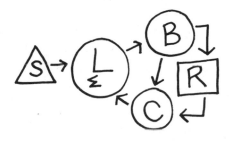

Alice cleared her throat. "No offense to you and your consultant, Will, but I don't see how understanding the concept of someone's learning history is going to create a quantum change."

I wasn't sure I did either, but it was all I had. "Are you kidding me? If we get the scorpion to stop stinging, and we get the frog and the scorpion to cross the river safely, that's a quantum change." Eyes moved skyward, and heads were scratched. "Anyway, we're not done yet. We've got more to talk about before putting these ideas into practice and creating some real change." I stood up and went over to the whiteboard.

"As we discussed yesterday, this is what describes the cycle of behavior. Specific behaviors give us the results we want, or keep us from getting them. So, what we need to do is to influence people's behavior, increasing the behaviors we want and decreasing the ones we don't. Everybody with me? ok—how do we do that?"

Alice eventually came to my rescue. "Through consequences. If we put in place the right consequences, that should affect behavior."

Mark went back to looking how he'd looked for most of the previous day: unhappy. "So, what, we give people electric shocks every time they do something wrong, like in *One Flew over the Cuckoo's Nest?* Maybe we should put dog collars on everyone."

Martha had warned me that some people would react this way, so I was prepared. "That's looking at consequences only as a nega-tive thing, Mark. We do tend to put a negative spin on the word. Remember that old game show *Truth or Consequences?*" Nobody bit. "Hosted by Bob Barker?" More blank stares. "You people are so out of touch," I chided. "But it doesn't matter. The premise of the show was that the contestants either answered a question correctly or there would be a consequence: something silly or embarrassing would happen to them. Which pretty much sums up how the word most often gets used—to describe something bad. But the word isn't inherently negative *or* positive. 'Consequence' simply means a result or an effect. In our model, it's what happens to a person after an action or a behavior. If I had a better word, I'd use it.

"Anyway—the consequences affect the behavior, via our learning history, and the behavior affects the result, so we need to think more about consequences. Specifically, how do we use them to get more of the behavior that gives us the result that we want, and less of the behavior that gives us the results we don't? Everyone good?" The resounding silence might have indicated a lack of enthusiasm, but it was too late to turn back.

"Let's start with some simple stuff," I suggested. "Stu, what was the consequence of you touching those glowing coals in the fire?"

"Extreme pain, followed by blisters and scarring."

Alice shuddered. "I thought you said consequences didn't have to be negative? So why are we starting with pain and scarring?"

"I did say that," I conceded, "and you're right. Maybe that wasn't the best starting point. In fact, let's talk a little more about structure, and then we'll get to examples, OK?" I turned to the whiteboard and wrote:

I had to hope the next part of Martha's diagram would hold their attention. "Practically speaking, we're trying to do one of two things: either we want *more* of a behavior that gives us the result we want"—I pointed to the upper arrow—"or we want *less* of a behavior that is giving us a result that we don't." I indicated the descending arrow. "Off the top of your heads, what might we do to get more of a particular behavior?"

"You attract more bees with honey than with vinegar," said Amanda. She glanced around the table. "What? That's what my grandmother used to say after I smacked my sister."

"I thought it was flies, not bees," said Stu.

"Hey," said Amanda, "it's my granny's saying. Take it up with her. Plus, who actually *wants* to attract flies?"

I smiled. "Sure, we'll go with that. Basic principle number one, as illustrated by the folksy saying 'If you give people a reward for a particular behavior, it tends to increase the frequency of that behavior.' We can use a fancy term for that reward, too: we're going to call it 'reinforcement.' If we reinforce a behavior, we're rewarding the behavior to get more of it. And reinforcement can be any consequence that a particular person finds positive or rewarding. That gets us into some weird stuff, which we'll talk about in a minute. For now, we can indicate reinforcement on our picture like this."

"The 'R' stands for 'reinforcement,' of course, and I put the little plus sign there to show that it's positive. I put the 'R' near the top to show that as we increase the reinforcement, we increase the behavior."

I paused and looked around the table. Nobody had fallen asleep yet, which was a good sign. "Now we ask the opposite question: what if we want to *decrease* a behavior? Or even get rid of it? How do we do that?"

"Beatings?" suggested Stu.

"Taser?" said Amanda.

"Put 'em on the rack," said Luigi.

"Poke them with knitting needles," added Leslie.

My management team were a sadistic bunch. "Those are all examples of one generic thing," I said. "I have to say, you're creeping me out a little with how quickly you're coming up with them. But they're all examples of what we call punishment, obviously. Punishment is the term we'll use to describe a consequence that a person finds negative or unpleasant. And as with reinforcement, the key is that a specific *individual* finds it unpleasant." I added to the diagram.

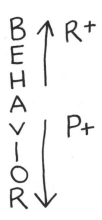

"Just like with reinforcement, I put a little plus sign by the 'P,' because increasing punishment has the effect of taking us down toward the bottom end of the arrow—it decreases behavior."

"Hang on," Mark said, looking smug. "Why is the 'P' near the middle instead of at the very bottom? Are you going to tell us there is something more powerful than punishment for getting rid of a behavior?"

I nodded. "Well spotted, Mark. You're getting a bit ahead of things, but we'll come back to your point. Sticking with punishment for a minute, if we wanted to illustrate this with Stu's example, we could say that he found staring at the glowing coals very *reinforcing*." I tried to put the word in verbal italics as I said it. "He thought touching the coals would be even more reinforcing. But it's probably safe to say he found picking up the glowing coals very *punishing*."

Stu concurred, making a joke of it. "I'm still in therapy to get over my fear of fire."

"Sure, Stu. Thanks for sharing." I paced a bit in front of the whiteboard to give myself time to review what Martha had told me about the remaining concepts. "We have to add two final ideas to our structure here to really capture what drives behavior," I told the group. "Initially, these don't seem quite as straightforward as the earlier ones. But after you think about them for a bit, they make a lot of sense. The first one is the simpler one, and we're going to call it 'extinction.'"

"Is this where the meteorite hurtles down from space and leaves a big smoking crater where the Hyler plant used to be? Kinda like a dinosaur thing?" asked Leslie. It was nice to get a little comic relief.

"It's a funny thing," I said. "When we're doing this kind of analysis, we often don't think carefully enough about what each individual will find rewarding. We tend to assume that if we personally find something rewarding or reinforcing, then everyone does too. That's a dangerous assumption, though, when you're talking about changing behavior. The last concept speaks to that. Sometimes when we're dealing with a behavior that we don't want, and we really analyze the situation, we discover the person is engaging in that behavior because they're getting some kind of reward for it. It might be a completely unintended reward, since their behavior is causing bad results, but nevertheless, they're getting rewarded, so they keep on engaging in the 'wrong' behavior. If we don't understand the pattern of reinforcement, we may inadvertently keep rewarding them for the behavior we don't want, and we're completely puzzled about why the behavior keeps happening."

I looked around the room. "The simplest example I can think of comes from my own kids. Our son, Jake, used to do a thing at bedtime where he would cry and fuss and have a big hissy fit about going to bed. We'd react with a bit of a tantrum ourselves, which only made things worse. At one point, Jenny's mom suggested that instead of engaging in the big fight at bedtime, we just leave the room when Jake started his little freak-out. It didn't feel like the right thing to do, but finally we got so frustrated we tried it. And amazingly, it worked."

Leslie, who had a couple of teenaged kids, was nodding. "I've been there, and I can tell you exactly what was happening—you were reinforcing Jake's tantrums. You might have thought you were punishing him by yelling at him, or whatever you guys did, but he was getting reinforced, to use your term, through all the attention you were giving him. That increased his bedtime behavior, which increased your attention, and things just got worse. Looking at your diagram on the whiteboard, what you did was to take away the reward for his tantrums, and the result was that the behavior stopped."

I could see that what Leslie said was registering with the team. That was the reinforcement that *I* needed to keep going. "Stopped isn't quite right," I said, "because it took us a while to do things consistently. But as we gradually saw that he was finding all the fuss rewarding, and we removed the reward for his behavior, it did finally die out. Or, to use the technical term, and to refine Leslie's dinosaur analogy, Jenny and I used 'extinction' to reduce and eventually eliminate the behavior we didn't want." I turned to the whiteboard and wrote:

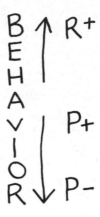

People were looking a little baffled when I turned back to the group.

"Another *P*? In what universe does the word extinction start with a *P*? Amanda asked. "I'm confused."

"Extinction is the removal of a positive consequence, or reward, in order to decrease a behavior," I explained. "That isn't as intuitive as the whole punishment and reward scheme, but it's a really important part of understanding why people do what they do. We may be rewarding behaviors we don't want in some situations, without even being aware of it.

"According to our trusty consultant, while the first 'P' stands for 'punishment,' the second 'P' with the minus sign is supposed to be a mnemonic for 'positive rewards reduced.' I'm told this is also the standard terminology for it. We can make it an 'E' later if you want. Ultimately it doesn't matter what letter we use, so long as we all have the same understanding about what it means."

Amanda shook her head. "Let's leave it for now, if that's the normal way to show it. But I do find it a little confusing."

I nodded. "Fair enough. If we start having problems with the 'P' minus, we'll change it."

"All this talk about the letter *P* has been working on my subconscious," Luigi said. "How about we take a little break so I can take care of that problem?" There were chuckles around the room as everyone stretched, pulled out cell phones, and made their way out to use the facilities. I took the opportunity to zip down to the lunchroom and buy some more doughnuts from the vending machine. Five minutes quickly became fifteen, and I finally had to chase people down to get them back to the boardroom.

"So, as I said before the break, there is one more thing to talk about. But before we do that, let's do a quick review, shall we, class?" No one seemed to find my professorial tone particularly amusing. "Consequences drive behavior. Positive consequences or rewards for a behavior—what we're calling reinforcement—increase the occurrence of a behavior. A negative consequence, or punishment as we're calling it, will decrease the occurrence of a behavior. Another way to decrease the occurrence of a behavior is to remove the reward for it, and we call this extinction." I watched the faces around the room, and then did my best impression of Don Henley. "Are you with me so far?" No one understood my clever Eagles reference, but I pushed on, undeterred.

"We're ready for the final concept and this is the one that's most confusing to me, probably because of the name: negative reinforcement."

"Isn't that just the same thing as punishment?" Alice asked.

"That's the confusing thing," I said. "It sounds like punishment. But negative reinforcement is actually a situation in which people avoid an unpleasant consequence by engaging in a certain behavior."

Sheila laughed. "You're describing my childhood! Everything I did as a kid seemed to revolve around not getting punished. Doing well at school, being quiet around my Nana when she was napping, learning to use my chopsticks properly so that I didn't get my knuckles rapped—it was all about avoiding getting yelled at."

I smiled at the murmurs of agreement from the others. "That's why it's so important that we understand the concept of it. A lot of what we do every day we do simply to avoid the bad stuff. Classic example: our law enforcement system is based on the idea of people behaving properly to avoid an unpleasant consequence." I went to the whiteboard and added our fourth concept:

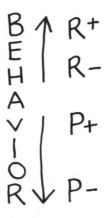

"The 'R' with the minus sign is the symbol we use for negative reinforcement," I explained.

Stu said, "I don't know about everyone else, but I can't help thinking 'punishment' when you say 'negative reinforcement.' Really what we're talking about is punishment avoidance, right?"

I shrugged. "Yep, that's it. Like I said, it doesn't matter what letter we assign it, so long as we know what we mean. What were you thinking?"

"How about 'A' for 'avoidance'?" Leslie suggested. "Not that I'm 100 percent sure I get this yet, but negative reinforcement sure sounds confusing to me, too."

It looked to me as if there was general agreement, so I went to the whiteboard and erased the "R" and put in an "A":

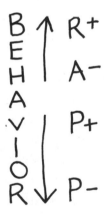

"Look," I said. "Now we have a cool acronym for the whole thing: RAPP!"

Stu grabbed a doughnut from the vending machine batch I'd supplied. "Rap on, man. I'm worried I'm already forgetting what they mean."

I put the marker in the tray under the whiteboard and sat back down at the table. "OK. There are a few other things we need to cover before we start thinking about how we're going to apply this stuff, so bear with me. The first thing has to do with the way consequences work, both for the person experiencing them and the person providing them. If we're trying to encourage a specific behavior, what's the most powerful way to do that?"

"It's back to Amanda's bee comment," said Stu. "If you reward someone for doing something, that encourages them to do it again."

"Sure," I said. "It's intuitive, and it's been proven in studies." I'd never seen any studies myself, but I had to trust Martha on that. "OK. What if we want to *discourage* a particular behavior? What's the best way to do that?"

Luigi was the first to answer. "Well, punishment, obviously. If someone is doing something you don't like, punishing them will discourage them pretty fast."

Leslie shook her head. "I don't know if I agree with that, Luigi. You don't have young kids, do you? Punishment has a big impact the first time around, but it wears off quickly, and then people start getting resentful and angry about it. And by 'people,' I mean my kids. I don't dole out any punishment at work."

Amanda smirked. "I'm not sure about that, Leslie. I've walked by the conference room when some of your sales meetings are going on, and it seems to me I've heard the occasional raised voice and loud comment coming from you."

Leslie feigned a look of surprise. "That's called motivating people. Salespeople like to be yelled at. I'm actually rewarding them!"

I decided to jump in. "However you feel about her loud voice, Leslie's right: punishment is good in the short term, but it loses its effect very quickly. In fact, it's recommended—" by Martha, of course; I had no other source on this "—that punishment be used only sparingly, and only in extreme situations where the behavior you're trying to get rid of is dangerous to the person or the people around them. Like when a kid throws something at another kid, or doesn't wait for the light to change before crossing the street."

"Or when you've got an equipment operator coming to work drunk," said Luigi. "You gotta take that stuff seriously and do something that will have an immediate impact. But what you're saying goes against how I was raised, Will. My dad used to spank me once a week and tell me he did it because if I wasn't doing something bad, I was thinking about it." Luigi paused and looked around the room. "Not that I'd recommend that as a way to raise kids."

"My dad was like that too. So how did that work out in the long run, Luigi?"

Luigi thought for a second and then said, "I stopped being scared of being spanked, and as I got older, I had to pretend it hurt so that my dad would think it was working. When I got too big to spank, he grounded me instead, but I'd just sneak out of my bedroom window."

"That illustrates the point nicely," I said. "Concentrating on the punishment side of the equation is about getting rid of things you don't like, instead of encouraging the behavior you do. Punishment is way overused, but it ends up having very little effect. Which is not to say that if one of your guys comes to work drunk, Luigi, you don't need to do something significant. It just means we've got to think very carefully about when punishment makes sense, and about where we focus our effort: on the behaviors we don't want, or on the ones we do." I pointed at the whiteboard. "When we're talking about reducing or eliminating behaviors, extinction is actually a better long-term solution."

Sheila said, "Explain that one again? I didn't quite get it the first time."

"Sure," I said. "And it's a good reminder of the fundamental principle we've got to keep in mind at all times when we're trying to change behavior: people do the things *they* find rewarding or reinforcing." Martha had stressed this was something the whole team needed to understand; otherwise, the framework wouldn't be very helpful.

Amanda spoke up. "Yeah, you've said that, Will. But why is it such a big deal?"

I took a sip of coffee as I carefully considered my response. "This is a delicate point, guys, and it's something that can get in the way of our success. On the surface, the idea that people do what they find rewarding isn't difficult. But as I said, we make a lot of assumptions about what people will find rewarding, what they should find rewarding, and how that compares to what we personally find rewarding. That all takes us into the territory of noble traits like selfishness."

"So, what are you saying?" Leslie asked. "How does this affect Hyler? Or the scorpion problem?"

Stu jumped in. "He's saying that we like to *think* we do things for highfalutin reasons, but when it comes right down to it, what we care about is what makes us happy in the moment."

Mark was clearly uncomfortable with this. "That's pretty hard to believe. Will, are you saying that people aren't capable of doing something for the right reason or because it's the right thing to do, even if it makes things harder for themselves? I don't buy that."

Martha had warned me that things could quickly go south at this particular juncture. I started to respond, but then Stu came to the rescue. "Look," he said, "let's leave the deeper philosophical discussions for sometime when we're not in imminent danger of losing our jobs. Everyone cool with that? Will is presenting some ideas that may be able to help us. We all know it would be crazy to keep doing what we're doing if we want different results. Remember way back when Will brought in a whole new approach to projects at Hyler? We had to buckle down then and try something different, and this situation is the same. Will is trying to show us a way forward, and we've got to trust him on this. Higher-order philosophical questions of our place in the universe will just have to wait. Unless someone else has a better idea, I propose we move forward and talk about the practical aspects of this."

I pretended to wipe away a tear. "Thanks, Stu. That was a very nice show of support."

Stu snorted. "Don't let it go to your head, Will. Believe me, if I had a better idea, we'd be doing that. All this talk about reinforcement and punishment conjures up images of rats in mazes. But I can also see the logic in it. And at this point, what have we got to lose?"

"Gee," I said. "My heart is lukewarmed. I appreciate the faint praise."

Amanda waved her hand in the air. "Uh, excuse me, are we done getting all sentimental and mushy? I'm with Stu: your ideas about performance and reinforcement make sense while still making me slightly uneasy. The real question is, what do we do now?"

ELEVEN

MARTHA GETS THE UPDATE

I ROCKED A LITTLE faster as Will got to this point in his story. I didn't want to show it, of course (curmudgeonly is my signature style), but I was excited by his progress. "Yes? So then what happened?"

"We broke for lunch. I'd had them in the conference room for close to two hours. We had to take a serious breather."

I pulled out my pipe and tobacco and started filling the bowl. Will's eyes went as wide as saucers.

"Martha, what are you doing?" he whispered.

"What does it look like? And why are you whispering?" I finished tamping the tobacco, put the pipe between my teeth, and proceeded to light it. It was having the desired effect; Will was doing a good impression of having an apoplectic fit.

"Because you're not supposed to be smoking that thing anymore!" he whispered fiercely. "It's not good for you! You were just in the hospital coughing up a lung!"

I laughed, then took a deep drag and carefully blew three smoke rings at Will. They were rather well formed, if I do say so myself, and the minimal breeze meant that they drifted perfectly right to their target: Will's open mouth. He coughed slightly. "Willie," I said, "I'm 102 years old. You have no idea what that means. Nor could you. After my last trip to the hospital, I decided it was time to get back to living my life the way I want. I may have only another fifteen or twenty years left to me, and I want to enjoy them."

Will was shaking his head. "No, no, no! You having another coughing fit and croaking right here on the porch would only be the half of it. If Jenny or Joanne find out you were smoking and I didn't do anything about it, I won't have another fifteen or twenty *minutes* left. They still think I was letting you do something shady when you started in with the coughing that landed you in hospital."

I took another puff and sighed contentedly. "You're welcome to try wrestling it away from me, Willie. But you'd be taking away an old woman's last pleasure." I smiled at him, confident that he wasn't going to go down that path. "But you're getting distracted. Before my granddaughter kills you for letting me smoke, tell me what happened after your lunch break."

Will stared at the pipe for a few more seconds, and then shrugged. "Either way, I can't win. If I wrestle you to the ground and take that thing away, I'm sure something else bad will happen." He settled resignedly into the porch swing and continued his story.

"So, putting the model out in front of the group, the next part seemed pretty easy. Like you told me, the good thing about this approach to understanding performance is that most people find it easy to relate to once they stop and think. By the time everyone came back from lunch, they were already getting more comfortable with the concepts.

"It started with Stu. He's always the practical one, and he does a good job of bringing us back to reality on a regular basis. As soon as we got back from lunch, Stu said, 'OK, Will, before we start talking about Hyler, I think we should talk about the frog and the scorpion again. Let's do a little practice run at applying this.' Everyone agreed. We'd all struggled with the mystery of why the scorpion stings the frog, so we dove right in. We identified the desired result as both frog and scorpion getting safely across the river, and we identified the positive reinforcement as being different for the two characters. For the frog, he was going to feel good about helping someone. And the scorpion needed to get across to go visit his mother, so he'd find that reinforcing."

I raised an eyebrow and blew another smoke ring. "He had to visit his mother?"

Will laughed. "We invented a bit of a backstory, OK? The scorpion's mother was sick, and he wanted to go see her. Anyway, we saw the desired behavior as being a couple of things: For Froggy, it was swimming the scorpion across the river. For the scorpion, it was *not* stinging the frog. So what happens? The scorpion stings the frog, they both drown, and we don't get the result we want."

"I'm familiar with the story," I said drily.

Will ignored me and carried on. "But here was the interesting part. How could this new model possibly explain the scorpion effectively committing suicide? It just didn't make sense. It was Amanda who finally hit on it. She said, 'Guys, here's what we're missing: stinging things is reinforcing for the scorpion. Highly,

highly reinforcing! That's why he does it. It's so reinforcing for him, and he gets such an immediate charge out of it, that it clouds his brain as to the long-term consequences. He's not thinking about drowning, he's thinking about feeling good.'

"Well, that set off a loud discussion, since we were effectively arguing about the contents of a joke. Some people wanted to talk about the physical makeup of a scorpion and hypothesize about what the physiological reaction is when it stings. Others claimed that since scorpions in real life only sting in self-defense, this wasn't a legitimate example. Turns out Amanda knows something about the spider and scorpion family, and she pointed out that this is incorrect; scorpions do in fact sting to kill prey. Once again, it was practical Stu who got us back on target. 'Here's the key,' he told us. 'We don't need to know exactly why the scorpion finds stinging reinforcing. We don't know and can't know his *learning history*, the term the model uses. Like Will said, someone's learning history is a bit of a black box. We need to recognize that it exists, because it allows us to think about adding new experiences to it that may help shape new behaviors, but in the end, all we care about is what behavior happens. The scorpion says that stinging is 'in his nature,' which is shorthand for saying he finds it reinforcing. That's all we need to know. That, and the fact that it's such a powerful reinforcer for him that he'd rather sting now and drown in two minutes than *not* sting and avoid drowning. So, if we know that stinging is such a big reinforcer for the scorpion, how do we change the situation to change the behavior so that we get a different result?'"

I nodded approvingly, taking another puff on my pipe. "Go on, Willie."

"Leslie was the first one to jump in with an idea. 'We've already talked about Kevlar armor being too heavy, but what about some fancy new material that's lighter, some kind of armor the frog can wear when he's transporting the scorpion so he's protected from getting stung?' 'I hear what you're saying," Alice replied, 'but think about it—if Froggy has to be outfitted with armor, our costs just went up. Plus, what if the frog can't swim as well all suited up? Suddenly crossing the stream takes twice as long. That doesn't seem like the best solution.'

"Luigi pointed out, 'But we already talked about how the armor is exactly the same as the impact posts. We're not really dealing with the behavior, we're just trying to find a way to make it so the behavior doesn't hurt the frog. But we aren't trying to change the scorpion's behavior.'"

Will took a sip of his beer, then continued. "At that point I took the opportunity to give them more background on how things work, just the way you said. I explained that the best way to encourage a behavior is an immediate, powerful reinforcer, delivered every time the behavior occurs. And that if we want someone to give up a behavior that gives the person that kind of reward, it's an almost impossible request. I used your example of people who are drug addicted and how they'll make just about any bad decision to get their next fix because it's such an immediate and powerful reinforcer. We talked about the relative strength of reinforcement for encouraging a behavior versus punishment for discouraging a behavior, and I explained again how extinction and avoidance work. Sheila jumped on that in the context of the scorpion by asking, 'Is there a way we could make stinging less reinforcing for the scorpion?'

"Somebody suggested punishing the crap out of the scorpion whenever he stings, but we quickly discounted that: once the scorpion's stung someone, it's too late. 'We could Taser the scorpion every time he does it,' someone else said, 'but then we're still losing frogs until the punishment starts working. Plus, for the time it's working, the scorpion is doing that "A-" thing on the model: avoidance.' Luigi went back to the earlier example we'd discussed. 'And there's always the possibility that once the scorpion gets used to the punishment, he'll go back to his old stinging ways.'"

I noticed I'd started rocking faster again. I can't believe I still get excited about these simple principles of human behavior, but I do. Or more accurately, I get excited about other people discovering them. "So what happened next?" I said.

"We struggled with that for a while until Stu said, 'How about this: what if we stop transporting scorpions on frogs across rivers?' Everyone looked at him like he'd grown a third eye. But he persisted. 'Seriously, people. That's one of the advantages of looking at the world through this performance management lens Will has introduced. It allows us to understand what's driving the behavior we're getting. Not every situation can be fixed with a simple tweak. In this case, maybe the solution is not to put scorpions on frogs' backs, because the reinforcers in that situation give us a behavior and a result that are unacceptable. In other words, if we can't figure out how to substitute reinforcers, add extinction, or use punishment effectively, then maybe we change the situation to one where we can provide reinforcement for the right behavior. And Bob's your uncle.'"

Will stopped to take a breath, and I smiled. "I like this Stu fellow. I remember I liked him the last time we talked about him, years ago. I bet someone is very happy to have him as a son-in-law."

Will looked exasperated, and I suppressed a little giggle. "Maybe it was me who said that about changing the situation; I don't remember," he said. "Regardless, that got everyone thinking and talking. The fact that understanding what was driving the situation meant we'd have to rethink the whole thing actually made the frame-work more appealing. I guess you could say that everyone found it *reinforcing.*" If Will was expecting me to smile at his little joke, he must not have been paying attention to how our relationship worked.

He went on. "So, having solved the scorpion problem, we decided it was time to tackle something work related, something that would have the most impact on Hyler going income positive in the shortest amount of time. Several people wanted to tackle operational issues up front. I let the discussion go for a while, and then I suggested we start with sales. Leslie was grumpy about it. 'Sure,' she said. 'Why not pick on sales? We're the only thing that's keeping this boat afloat right now, but we're always the ones you go to when you need more.' I reminded her of the analysis we'd done on sales. 'The issue isn't the sales group's effort,' I reassured her. 'It's the mix of what we're selling and the price we're selling it at. Right now, we've got a great example of ineffective performance management in action. We're giving immediate, positive reinforce-ment to the sales team to sell stuff that we lose money on.'

"Leslie was having none of it. 'You start taking away the sales-person's ability to discount the price, you're gonna see a huge drop in the company's revenue. You tell someone what to sell, same thing. How is that going to get us into positive territory with income?'

"Luckily, I had other people willing to step up to the plate. Amanda was one of them. 'Listen to what you're saying, Leslie. You're saying it's better to lose money on every sale than to sell less, or nothing, and not lose money. That's a recipe for disaster if I've ever heard one.'"

Will was really warming to his story, and I had to admit it was holding my attention. "Just like you and I talked about, Martha, we started by mapping out the existing situation. The funny thing was, we didn't learn anything new. The only surprise was that we'd kept doing things that way for as long as we had.

"The essentials were simple. For as long as anyone could remember, Hyler salespeople had been incented based on the total sales they generated. When the recession hit and things started going bad, the focus on volume increased. Without really thinking about it, the company had become completely focused on pushing product out the door, while losing track of how that affected the bottom line. As a result, we had given the sales team a free hand with discounts, and lots of leeway to sell whatever they could get the customer to buy."

I felt I needed to step in there and share some of my own experience with Will. "Don't be too hard on yourselves, Willie. It's a pretty common problem. People start thinking it's better to keep the factory doors open and make things at a loss than to simply shut down. And that may be a viable strategy in the short term, but you need to explore the alternatives."

Will nodded. "It does have a kind of logic to it, but only if you don't think too carefully about the implications for the medium and long term. In our case, this had been going on for years. Funny thing was, if you looked at Hyler's numbers at the top line, they didn't decline nearly as much as you would have expected. But what was declining, in fact going negative, was our profitability." Will took out a pad of paper. "When our group did the analysis, we determined that in the current situation we had this." He wrote for a minute, then showed me what he had.

Result = Sales volume steady, Hyler losing money
Consequence (to the salesperson) = positive, relatively
immediate, monthly commission checks

Behavior = discount prices, promises of aggressive
(expensive) delivery times, don't worry about profitability
Learning History = the organization rewards sales at any cost
Stimulus = every sales meeting, Leslie and the company
focusing on revenue

He set the pad down on the table. "It was obvious when we talked it through. We'd made a conscious choice to reinforce our sales-people for selling, and they were responding beautifully. Equally obvious was that we had to change that situation. Amazingly, though, even after we'd identified the problem, there was still resistance to the idea, with Leslie and Mark at the forefront. 'Look,' they told me, 'we've got a factory here, employees. That's a cost for Hyler, and basically it's fixed. You want those people to sit around idle? How's that going to make us profitable?' Luckily, Stu and the rest took the other side. 'If our current, money-losing situation is analogous to us being on fire, then incenting the salespeople to sell below our cost is like pouring gasoline on it!' That one was Sheila's. I thought it was a good way of looking at things. In the end I had to weigh in with a harsh reality check. I told them, 'We used to run three shifts a day, seven days a week. We've cut that back to two shifts a day, five days a week. Maybe it needs to go lower than that. Maybe at the moment we can only support one shift plus some overtime. And maybe in the short run that means laying people off. But if we keep going like we're going, *everyone* is going to get laid off, and Hyler will be done.' There was some unhappiness over my bluntness, but everyone recognized it for what it was: the truth."

I smiled. "Careful with that, Willie. You keep falling back on telling the truth and you'll get a reputation for being a crusty old curmudgeon. Just like me." Will has this need to be loved by his people, and I couldn't resist giving him a little poke.

"Our next task was to map out what we needed to do differently," Will continued, "and everyone saw pretty clearly that we'd have to incent the salespeople based on profitability, not volume. If we were losing money on it, we didn't want to be selling it.

"There was a fair bit of discussion, almost all of it pointless, about how we'd track and measure that. It was pointless, because we already have the systems in place to do that. I think everyone wanted to talk about tracking and measuring because it was something concrete. What no one wanted to talk about was the conversation we'd need to have with the sales staff. And then we got a bit of a shock: Leslie said she was out. I asked her what she meant by that, and she said she wasn't prepared to go back to the sales staff and tell them the commission structure was changing. That threw us all for a loop, and that's when I called the meeting for the day."

"Did I ever tell you about how I came to be involved in performance management?" I asked Will. He shook his head. "It was in the '50s, well after the war. My husband and I had started to expand our business in the postwar boom, and we were doing a lot of interesting things. But we ran into a problem on the shop floor of one of our factories. We had converted a production line that had been making electronic components for military aircraft into one making components for an exciting new technology called the transistor radio. Ever heard of those?" I didn't bother to wait for an answer. "Just think of them as the smartphone of the '60s. In those days, automation wasn't as advanced, and most of the assembly work was done by hand. By real people. But unlike your situation, our problem was that we couldn't keep up with demand.

We were in danger of losing contracts simply because we couldn't get production up to the levels we needed. We tried a variety of things, including an incentive pay scheme, better training of workers, better benefits. What happened? Our productivity actually went *down* instead of up.

"One night in the midst of all of this, we had an old friend over to our house for dinner. My husband had gone to school with Burrhus, and we'd kept in touch over the years. Once in a blue moon the three of us would get together for dinner and talk about things. Burrhus was a great person to have a conversation with—he was so interesting and into so many things. He was a college professor, which gave him lots of opportunity to explore new ideas. In fact, not long before that particular dinner, he'd gotten an appointment at one of the fancy eastern Ivy League schools based on the work he was doing in psychology.

"Our factory problems came up over dinner, and we ended up discussing them in detail. At some point, Burrhus suggested we ought to look at performance in a slightly different way. He talked me through the basic principles I've imparted to you, and he later made several visits to our factory floor to help us put some of these ideas in place."

Will, always the smartass, asked, "Is Burrhus available to come help us?"

"He didn't make it past eighty-six," I said tartly. "So you're stuck with me. But back then Burrhus was a real whirlwind. Once he'd brought us up to speed on the performance framework, we started to apply it at the factory. And what do you suppose we found?"

Will answered quickly. He was really taking to this stuff. "I'm assuming you discovered you were reinforcing the wrong behaviors, or what you thought was reinforcing turned out to have no impact."

I noticed my pipe had gone out. "You're not as dumb as you look, Willie. Or not nearly as. Yes, we found out those things and more. One of the most interesting things we learned was that money isn't always the prime motivator for people."

Will didn't look surprised. "It all seems intuitive once you spell out the basic framework. I feel as if Tyler is on the verge of something with regard to reinforcement. My worry is that we won't be able to get the results we need in time."

I spent a moment relighting my pipe, and then continued talking. "I wouldn't worry too much about a complete turnaround, Willie. Your biggest problem is going to be showing a trend in the right direction. But if you pick the right behaviors to focus on, the ones that really drive the business, change can be almost immediate." I paused for a moment to let this sink in. "Don't forget that you have to be clear about what people actually find reinforcing. In my experience, one of the most important things is feedback."

Will raised an eyebrow. "Meaning what?"

"Information, Willie, clearly spelled-out information about how they're doing. And keep it simple—you can show people a graph, a picture, even a crayon drawing as long as it lets them know how they're doing. Let me give you an example: why do you think we keep score in a baseball game?"

Will looked at me suspiciously, clearly expecting a trap. "So we know who won?"

"And why do we care about that?" I asked him.

He looked more suspicious. "Well... what's the point of playing a sport if you don't keep score? Isn't the objective to win? No one would care about baseball if we didn't keep score."

I nodded in agreement. "That's not the most eloquent way I've heard the idea expressed, but you're on the right track. People who play sports and people who watch sports care about the outcome. Yes, people go out there and play for exercise, or to develop their ability at 'teamwork,' whatever that means. But when it comes down to it, take away the score, and you tell me how popular baseball would be."

Will shrugged. "Not very. There wouldn't really be any point. You play a sport because you care about winning."

I blew another perfect smoke ring. This one bounced off Will's forehead. "Funny thing, isn't it? We like sports because there are clearly laid out goals and objectives, and we get instant and ongoing feedback on how well we're doing at achieving those goals. As a result, we can see immediately how our behavior is affecting the outcome, positively or negatively. Win or lose, we come back to play the sport, or to watch it, over and over again. Sounds like we find the whole experience reinforcing, doesn't it?" Will nodded. "Now contrast that with work. We expect people to come to work and engage in activities that are not clearly related to any particular big-picture outcome. We give them very little feedback on their progress—that is, on whether a company is winning or losing, and we expect them to find all this motivating simply because we provide them with money. Moreover, that money is primarily associated with them showing up regularly for work, as opposed to doing anything in particular. Is it any wonder we have trouble getting people motivated about work?"

I could see Will's curiosity was piqued. "ok, so what kinds of things did you do to provide feedback for your employees?" he asked.

"Lots of simple things," I told him. "For people on the production line, we provided them with daily information about how much product we were putting through, the level of quality or number of defects that were found, the percentage of on-time orders that went out. We gave them the information on graphs and in pie charts, and when all else failed, in plain numbers. Over time, we figured out which indicators we needed to achieve to get the results we wanted. Then we trained everyone so they understood what behaviors they needed to engage in to drive the numbers we wanted. We tied a certain amount of pay to achieving those numbers, but we were pretty sure in the long run that wasn't the main reinforcer—the immediate information was. Which fits the framework I showed you, doesn't it? What's the most powerful way to influence behavior?"

Will looked at me and pretended to scratch his head. "Is this a test?"

I glared at him. "Answer the question."

"Immediate, positive reinforcement."

"Correct," I said. "And how do you get that if you pay someone every two weeks? We actually looked at paying more frequently, maybe even at the end of each shift. But we didn't end up doing it. You know why?"

"Too complicated and expensive?" Will suggested.

"Those were issues, yes. But the real reason was because we found we didn't have to. The immediate reinforcement received from the feedback did the trick. People liked knowing how their pay was tied to performance, and they seemed to appreciate being able to influence their wages, but when it came right down to it, making the graphs go in the right direction was their primary reinforcer." I took my pipe out of my mouth and pointed the stem at him. "Remember that, Willie, and don't wait for the next thing you tackle. Think about it for your sales team. They're not only about money either, you know."

Will looked uncertain. "I don't know, Martha. To hear Leslie tell it, money is the only thing that drives those folks."

I clucked my tongue. "Nonsense, Willie. You don't think your sales team gets reinforced every time they make a sale? You don't think they get reinforced by knowing the number of sales they make in a month? Sure, the sales are tied to money, but I suspect for a lot of them, reaching a certain number is the primary reinforcer. At some point, they're going to want to get paid for that. But make sure you don't depend only on the money. Give them feedback on the types of sales you want them to make, how many of those they're making, and how the numbers they're generating compare to last month's numbers and to each other's. All those things will be reinforcers for them, and they will in turn drive the right behavior. Assuming, of course," I looked over the top of my glasses at him, "you've picked the right behaviors to reinforce. Think about making work like a sport, Willie. Be sure people know the rules, know their roles, know the goals, and know how it's all measured. It's fairly straightforward, really."

Will continued to look uncertain and, if I was any judge (which I most certainly am), a little forlorn. "It feels overwhelming, Martha. So many behaviors, so many results, and trying to set up processes so people can get feedback . . ."

"Start simple, Willie, like you already have. Pick an area, something to begin with. Like sales. And don't expect things will go smoothly just because you've got an understanding of the framework. Change is hard, and it takes time. By the way, what happened in the end with Leslie?"

"She quit," he said.

I was starting to see why Will was looking so worried.

TWELVE

WILL IMPLEMENTS THE MODEL WITH THE SALES TEAM

I WAS PRETTY sure beads of sweat were visible on my forehead. It wasn't the first time I'd been sorry I didn't have much cranial hair anymore. When you've got a nice, thick head of hair, you can hide all sorts of things, not the least of which is how uncomfortable you're feeling.

"Don't give us that bullshit," Karl said loudly. "You don't think she talked to us? Leslie quit because she thinks you're about to screw the sales team."

I was standing in front of the entire Hyler sales force—twenty-three people including Karl, most of them middle-aged men, two of them younger and female. I smiled in a manner I hoped the team would later describe as "thinly." "Karl, isn't that what I just said? We had a difference of opinion about the direction we're going in. Leslie decided she didn't want to be part of it. She quit. I'm not happy about it, but that's what happened."

Karl smirked. "What about the part where she thinks you're going to screw the sales team?"

I spread my hands out in front of me, palms up. "That's where we disagree. I'm not going to screw the sales team. I'm going to change it. In the world we live in, I'm being paid to make those changes. What I'm *not* paid to do is to keep doing the same old thing and getting the same old results."

Karl looked around at his colleagues, then back at me. "C'mon, this is just the start, isn't it? You're here to shut this place down, move the production offshore somewhere, and send us all on our merry way, aren't you?"

Karl was starting to irritate me. Not to mention the fact that I was exceptionally tired of hearing that I was planning to move things offshore. "I've told you several times already that I'm here to do the opposite. I've also told you that means change."

"So we either live with it or we're gone too?" There were ominous rumblings around the room that made me think of the moment in a bar just before the fighting breaks out. I decided I'd better take some aggressive action.

"That's not what I'm saying at all, Karl. I'm saying you can be part of the change. You can also choose to believe that doing the same old things we've been doing, the things that have gotten us into this hole, are going to get us out. Is that the way you want to play it, Karl?" I was pleased to see him looking defensive.

"No, I'm not saying that." He tried another tack. "But why are you messing with *us*? We're the group that has held this place together for the last five years." There were murmurs of agreement from the group. "You look at the numbers we've made, despite the recession, and you'll know that we're not the problem."

I flipped the cover off the projector. A graph appeared on the screen. "In a way you're right. But not the way you think." I pointed to the graph. "See that? That shows our sales volume, by product line. It also shows the profitability of each product line. Tell me what you see."

Karl was cagey enough not to answer, but Samantha, one of the two women, spoke up. "Is that graph right? It says that we're doing our biggest volume in products that aren't making the company any money."

I nodded. "Correct. Except if you look closely, it's not that those products aren't making us any money. They are *costing* us money. For every unit of Windsailors we've moved in the last year, we've lost more than $1,000. We're selling this stuff below cost. And you guys are selling lots of it. What do you think that means?"

Karl was trying to stay ahead of me. "So there's your problem. The manufacturing guys have to do it cheaper. They have to get costs down."

I flipped to the next slide. "See that, Karl? That shows our manufacturing costs, by product, over the last five years. What do you see?"

Again Karl didn't answer, but Samantha did. "The costs have gone down."

I nodded. "That's correct. They have been going down. Not a ton, but down." I clicked through to the next slide. "What do you see there, Karl?"

Samantha answered again, as I now expected she would. "Seriously? Are you sure those numbers are right?"

I pointed at the screen. "The data isn't perfect, but it gives us a ballpark indication. See that line right there? That's our production cost over the last five years. The line below it is a rough estimate of the industry average. See how our line was much higher than average five years ago, but how it comes back down now and meets the average? What does that mean to you?"

Samantha said, "You're saying that our costs are competitive."

I nodded. "That's what I'm saying, all right. I'm saying we're in the ballpark. We can improve it, but our problem includes some issues with how we're selling our products. And those issues include the whole Hyler sales team." I clicked through to the next slide. "Here's one of the really important bits. I'm not saying any of this is the sales force's fault. I'm not saying that at all. In fact, I'm saying that you guys have been doing an unbelievable job."

Karl looked at me suspiciously. "Yeah, we know that."

I pointed at the slide on the screen. It said:

> Sales has been doing
> an unbelievable job.

I clicked, and the next few words slid onto the screen:

> Management is
> the problem.

Many people were looking confused by this point. "You guys have been doing exactly what we've asked you to do," I said, "and doing a great job of it. The problem is that we've been asking you to do the wrong thing. We've been asking you to move product at all costs. Regardless of price, delivery commitments, quantity, anything. You guys have been doing just that, and we've been rewarding you for it."

Karl jumped to his feet. "I knew it! You're here to cut our commissions! We're performing like we should, but we're the ones who have to take a bullet for the team, because we're successful."

"Karl," I said, trying to keep all trace of emotion out of my voice. "Please sit down and let me continue so you can see what I'm talking about." Reluctantly, Karl dropped back into his seat. "As I was saying, we've been rewarding you for that. With commissions, of course. But also with feedback. We give you lots of progress reports on how much product you're moving. We have competitions to see who can move the most. We do lunches for the top salesperson of the week, and we print up certificates for the people who move the most every month. Money is part of the reward, but if you really look at it, we're driving you guys in every way toward the holy grail of volume."

By now, I could see a few people nodding. I took a deep breath before continuing. "But as I said, the problem is that we've been asking you to do the wrong thing, which is to sell lots of stuff, regardless of any other consideration. In the beginning, when the recession hit, that made sense. We wanted to keep things running here, keep people employed, so we were willing to take some short-term losses to make that happen. But as you know, months have now stretched into years. We used to run three shifts a day, seven days a week. Now we run two shifts, five days a week. We've cut everywhere else, too, including the sales team. Despite the smaller sales force, you folks are selling more per person than we ever did in the old days. So, good for you.

"But now we've got to make some changes. And one of the major changes is in how we sell our products—how much, which products, and at what price. Because, like we just discussed, in our current model our sales success is translating directly into red ink on the bottom line. That's not something we can continue. So we're shifting our focus." I brought up the next slide. "Here's what we need to do."

> Focus on profitability,
> not volume

Karl scowled. "What did I tell you? This is just a fancy way of letting us know you're cutting our commissions."

I was taken aback when Samantha said, "Karl, would you shut up for a second? Don't you get it? If there's no Hyler, your goddamn commissions are going to be zero. We can't just expect that things are magically going to get better."

I resisted the urge to say thank you and kept talking. "Like the slide says, we have to start focusing on *profitability*, not simply volume. We have to sell our products at prices where we can make money, not simply at a level where customers are happy to buy them. Look at this." I brought up a slide showing retail margins over the last five years. "See that? Consumer prices for our products have dropped, but not that significantly, and the margins our wholesalers and retailers are making have actually increased. They're happily taking our lower prices, and they're doing fine, thank you very much. So that's where our change is coming, folks."

I went on to explain the new incentive program to the group. It was straightforward: from now on, we would pay commissions based on the profitability of a sale, not simply on the sale itself. We were changing all of the sales team reporting to get them thinking about profit, not just volume. We had also set things up so that if a salesperson was successful at selling things profitably, he or she could actually make more in commissions than previously. It wasn't a complicated shift, but I could see there was unease about the concept. Even Samantha looked a little nervous.

She said, "Will, I get where this is coming from. On paper, it makes sense. But what about the wholesalers and retailers we sell to? What if they won't buy our products if they can't get the same pricing we've been giving them? What then?"

"Yes, that's a worry," I agreed. "We don't know how the customers are going to react. Any time you change something, there's risk.

Our information on margins suggests we should be able to make it fly with them, but you never know. However, what we do know is this: if we keep losing money on every product we sell, we'll be out of business in a very short time."

Seeing all the worried faces in the room, I decided to try and lighten things up. "I even know a joke about this kind of situation. There's these two guys with suit shops in the garment district in New York. Times are tough, and they're both looking for ways to stay in the black. They're having coffee one morning before work, and one of them tells the other, 'I've got a plan, Fred. I know how I'm going to break out of this slump. I've got a great deal from my supplier in Hong Kong—he's sending me a huge shipment of Armani suits made in Bangladesh—only $205 a suit, right to my door. I'm going to have a massive blowout sale and put 'em all on for $200 a suit! Can you imagine? Armani suits for $200 each? People will be stampeding to my shop!' Fred looks at him and says, 'For $200? But they're costing you $205 each. How is that going to work?' The first guy says, 'Don't worry—I'm going to make it up on volume!'"

Nobody laughed, and I immediately regretted my decision to make a joke. "I'm sorry, that wasn't funny. I know this is a serious time, and I understand what this means to all of us. It means our jobs, and it means putting food on the table for our families. It affects me just like it does you. My kids are growing up in this community, just like yours. If there's no Hyler here, then I'm going to have to move. I don't want to do that, and neither do you. But if we're going to turn things around, we've got to try something different. Otherwise, it's guaranteed that we'll all be looking for new jobs." And with that, the meeting was over.

THANKFULLY, THE next day was not all doom and gloom.

"Will, you're going to want to see this." Luigi was standing outside my office door, holding a sheaf of papers.

"What's that?" I asked.

"Inventory reports. You know how we've been wondering what to do with that big batch of product we have out in warehouse C— some older-model Windsailors and other stuff? Well, look at this." He waved the papers at me.

I sighed. "Just tell me the bad news."

Luigi grinned. "For once, it's not bad news. It's a mistake in our favor. Apparently all the bitching I did about the inventory resulted in someone in accounting taking matters into their own hands."

"To do what?" I asked tiredly. "Set fire to it so we can collect the insurance money?"

"Better," promised Luigi. "They wrote it off. They took the product out of inventory and took the hit on income a couple of months ago."

My spirits immediately perked up. "So you're saying we've got a bunch of product here with no cost of goods sold attached to it?"

"Well," said Luigi, "technically there is a cost. It's just that we've already taken the hit for it."

By now I was smiling too. "So whatever we sell this stuff for now, it's all profit! This also explains some of our results a few months ago. Anyway, this is a small bit of good news for the sales team."

Luigi nodded. "And they sure need it. Those guys generally only come talk to me about how great they're doing, but after your meeting I've heard nothing but bitching. Hey, who do I talk to in sales now that Leslie's gone?"

"Talk to Karl," I advised him. "I don't know who we'll put in to replace Leslie yet."

Once Luigi was gone, I decided it was time to take a little drive. Tempted as I was to find a bar and ease my stress with a vodka decorated with a splash of cranberry juice, I was pretty sure that would end poorly. I talk big on the drinking side, but really I'm compensating for the fact that after one drink I'm usually ready for a long nap. I've always found a certain appeal in serious-looking men drinking Scotch as they ponder the weight of the world, but going for a drive has always been a more effective way for me to think things through.

Some people like to complain about the rain in the Pacific Northwest, and compensate for their snowy, twenty-below winters by pointing out "at least it's sunny." I think if you live with the rain long enough you come to appreciate its beauty and enjoy how the filter of the falling water softens the light and brings a feeling of calm.

Sure, and thinking crap like that is sometimes a helpful way of getting yourself through until the next sunny day which, quite frankly, always kicks a rainy day's butt.

My mood could have used a day that was glorious and unseasonably warm, with sunshine sparkling off Lake Hyler, enticing me to break out a Windsailor. I'd likely be dead from hypothermia twenty minutes after hitting the water, but it was nice to contemplate.

To say I was worried at that point was an understatement. I was plain, old-fashioned terrified. Moving into new territory with an idea is always a combination of excitement about the change and fear of failure, but this time around, it was on a whole new level. Which I guess wasn't unreasonable, given that the future of Hyler was riding on this performance management thing.

The next day I had scheduled a brainstorming session with Luigi and engineering to look for low-hanging fruit in production.

We were going to apply the same ideas to the situation, identify the right behaviors, and look at how we could change the reinforcement cycle to make it better. I wasn't convinced that our new approach to turning things around for the company was going to be enough. I felt like we should be doing something much more dramatic. The problem was, apart from closing the place down, I didn't have any ideas about what that more dramatic thing might be.

I had left the plant and was getting close to town. I drove past elm trees and stately old houses. I drove by picturesque fields in which horses were eating grass and cows were wandering about. I saw farmers on tractors and kids playing basketball in driveways. Through it all, one thought kept running through my head: it rains all the time in this part of the world! Man, was it gloomy and damp, and that was a perfect fit for the space inside my head. Well, I reflected, I bet it's sunnier in Indonesia.

THE NEXT day found me back at the front of the conference room, feeling an unpleasant combination of lack of confidence in what I was doing and apprehension about what I imagined would be hostility from the group I was facing. Happily, there were two friendly faces in the group: Sheila and Luigi were both there to help with the session. There was nothing to do but get started.

"Luigi has talked to you about what we're trying do, guys." Except for Sheila, everybody in the room was male. "We've done some piecemeal process improvement in the last couple of months, but today we're focused on finding things that will allow us to make more significant improvements. You all know what we're up against, and that the future of this plant is on the line. As a result, we can't keep doing the same old things; we've got to do things differently. That means we need to *think* about things differently, and that's what we're here to do today." This was greeted with an enthusiastic silence, along with a few yawns, sneezes, and various other voluntary and involuntary bodily noises. I tried to keep a hopeful look on my face as my eyes swept the room. A tumbleweed blew across the floor. A coyote howled in the distance.

Luigi stepped up. "Blaine, tell Will about your idea. You know, what you said to me yesterday when I told you guys about this session." A young man with a few days of beard growth shuffled to his feet. I took an immediate dislike to him, entirely based on the realization that my daughter might find him attractive. When Blaine spoke, he sounded respectful and more than half bright. I almost felt guilty for not liking him. Almost.

"It's the impact posts, Mr. Campbell. You want something easy, get rid of them."

I raised my eyebrows. "The impact posts? What do they have to do with anything? We're talking about cutting costs."

"Don't you be talking like that, Blaine," said a voice from the back of the room. Gary Minette stood up. "Those impact posts are there for our safety. You know how hard we had to fight the company to get 'em?" Gary, the president of the production workers' union, was a guy I hadn't had a lot of contact with. "The union won't stand for anything that puts workers at risk, so don't even go there."

Blaine wasn't fazed. "I'm not so sure they increase worker safety, Gary. I'd say they actually make it less safe around here. How many times a day does someone run into one of those poles?"

"Better a pole than a piece of equipment," Gary said heatedly. "Guys used to get injured all the time running into machines."

Luigi spoke up. "Pardon my French, Gary, but that's bullshit. Guys weren't running into machines all the time. There was one incident with Frank Rivers—"

Gary raised his voice to interrupt. "Who lost his left hand in the accident!"

"—with Frank Rivers, who we're pretty sure was drunk when he crashed."

"That was never proved!" yelled Gary.

Luigi yelled right back. "Because the union managed to get the blood test thrown out of court!"

Angry as he seemed to be on the surface, I couldn't help thinking that Gary was enjoying this. "Because the blood sample was taken while Frank was unconscious! You were on a witch hunt against Frank!"

Luigi was turning red. "Those frickin' impact posts were all political. Not only did you keep Frank out of jail and in the union, you cost us a pile of money putting in worthless equipment, all in the name of safety."

I knew a bit about the Frank Rivers situation; it was a real tragedy. It was even sadder that Frank had been in a car accident two years later and killed an elderly woman at a red light. Apparently the blood test had been allowed to make it to court that time. Frank was supposed to be eligible for parole in four more years.

"Wait, wait," I said, stepping in between Luigi and Gary. "Hang on for a minute. Let's leave the history lesson aside. That all happened before I arrived back here. Blaine, why are you suggesting we take out the impact posts?"

"They slow things down, Mr. Campbell. Before the posts went up, we could get the forklifts in next to the production equipment. Whether you were moving raw materials or partially finished product, you could slide the stuff in there right where the opera-tors needed it. Once they got going with the posts, we couldn't get anywhere near the equipment. So what happens now is, you drop the load by the impact posts, then you go and get a hand truck or dolly and shift everything over to where the guys need the stuff. It takes forever."

Luigi was nodding. "The kid's right, Will. It's hard to believe we haven't looked at this before. After the Rivers accident, we started building those posts as part of our collaboration with the union, but no one bothered to look at the impact on the produc-tion flow. We just got used to living with it. When things started getting tight, we squeezed everywhere we could, but we never looked at that. I guess everyone figured it was off limits because of the safety thing."

"It *is* off limits!" Gary piped up.

Luigi ignored him. "Yesterday, when I was talking to the guys, Blaine came up with this idea in about three seconds."

I looked at Blaine and decided that if he never met my daughter, I could learn to like him. "How much time do you think taking out the posts could save us?"

Blaine looked uncomfortable. "I'm not sure, Mr. Campbell. But I'm guessing there's a couple of hours of my time that could be saved in a shift."

Twenty-five percent? In one shift? I resisted a theatrically sharp intake of breath. "Luigi?"

"I ran some quick numbers last night," Luigi said, "and I think that's in the ballpark."

A thought hit me. "Supposing we could reduce the delivery time to the operators, is that going to help us? Is there demand for more throughput?"

Sheila chimed in. "Funny thing, Will—yes, there is. Remember how the sales guys have been promising customers these crazy delivery times? Well, this would affect that. Nobody really talks about it, but since we've cut back to two shifts we've been behind the eight ball to get product out the door. If we could cut the processing time and ship more quickly, there is demand for what we can produce."

I had a moment of indigestion as I thought about how we'd just changed the sales incentive program. What impact was that going to have on demand? I pushed the thought aside and followed up with another question. "What about the machine operators? What have they been doing while they're waiting for deliveries? Sitting idle?"

Blaine answered that one. "Depends on the guy. Some of them help us move stuff if they're waiting. Some of them go out for a smoke. You can tell who's helping and who's smoking by where work in process is piling up."

I thought Luigi's head was going to detach itself from his neck. "Once again, he's right, Will. That's exactly how it goes. In fact, you should be firing me and putting Blaine in charge. I can't believe we let this one go too."

Gary couldn't take it anymore. "I thought we were talking about safety. Those impact posts are there for a reason, and if you move even one of them, my guys are walking off the job. Let's see how that affects your production!"

His words caught the attention of the room. Everyone's eyes swung back to me, as if we were in a slow-motion tennis match. "You're threatening another wildcat strike?" I asked Gary. I tried to sound like Clint Eastwood, but with the lump in my throat I was pretty sure it was more like Burl Ives.

Gary nodded his head stubbornly. "Our contract gives us the right to refuse unsafe work. Period. End of story. You take out those posts, it's not safe."

"You know that if you go on strike, the plant will close down permanently? You'd put everyone here out of work?" I said.

Gary had the confidence of the self-righteous in his voice. "It's not me who'd be putting them out of work. Don't touch those posts, and everyone keeps on working."

Luigi had a good comeback for that, having clearly dealt with this before. "Take a pill, Gary. The contract says you can refuse unsafe work, but since there's no proof the impact posts have actually done anything, you're gonna have a hard time proving it's unsafe if they come out. In fact, I think the guys are going to appreciate their jobs getting a little easier."

Gary said something that sounded as if he was suggesting someone's mother was a trucker and stormed out of the meeting room. Things stayed silent until one of the older guys, whose name I couldn't remember, spoke up. "We're union members, but we're also workers. Blaine isn't the only one who's noticed the problem with the impact posts. Most of us thought it was stupid to put so many in in the first place. Not that anyone asked us. As long as we don't have a spike in accidents, we're all gonna be fine with this."

I tried not to sound too relieved. "I appreciate that," I started as I struggled to recall the guy's name. Corey? Conrad? "We're trying to make this operation feasible again, and we'll consider any suggestions you guys have."

Corey/Conrad spoke up again. "If you're serious about that, we've got a few more of them."

An hour and a half later, we had three other good ideas to take a hard look at. They concerned changes that had crept onto the factory floor in the name of various programs, including safety, without any clear objective—and definitely without considering the cycle of performance, punishment, and reward. The various schemes the company had put in place performed pretty much exactly as you would expect if you analyzed them with our new performance management framework: they weren't achieving the desired result. So many of the dysfunctional behaviors around the plant started making sense when you thought about them in terms of Martha's performance model. It was almost scary to see how often Hyler had done things that went directly against what the performance model would have suggested.

The following afternoon, Luigi and Sheila were in my office with a big stack of paper. "You've got a plan?" I asked them.

They nodded vigorously in unison. "We've got more than a plan, Will," said Sheila. "We've got hope!" She spread some pages in front of me, all covered with colorful graphs. "We got some great ideas from the guys yesterday. Even if we just tackled the impact posts, we'd be making great progress. But after you left the session, we discovered something else."

She stopped talking and looked at me. "Are you pausing for dramatic effect, or am I supposed to say something here?" I asked.

Sheila smiled. "Just for the drama. You know how we talked about information being a reward? In the model you presented?" She paused again.

I nudged her. "And...?"

"And that's the deal here." She rummaged through the papers she'd spread out and pulled out a graph. "See this? It's our lost-time accident stats. We used to post these in the lunchroom, many moons ago. Somehow we stopped doing it. Nobody remembers why. But here's the kicker: See how lost time decreases slightly over time? And see that point right there where it changes and starts to increase again? Guess what was happening then."

I thought for a minute. "The company started installing impact posts?"

Luigi jumped in. "Bingo! Give the man a prize. It turns out that the collisions between forklifts and posts created more downtime than before. But there's something even more important than that."

It was Sheila's turn again. "We stopped using the information about the accident rate! Hugh over in accounting kept collecting data and cranking out reports, but we didn't share them with anyone. Hell, we didn't even look at them ourselves. All those reports just went into a file somewhere and sat. Weird thing is, during that session with the guys, we learned *they* missed the information more than we did!"

Luigi continued. "They said they didn't feel like they had any idea how they were doing. Not just on accidents, but on everything. How was our production volume doing? Efficiency? Defect rate, all that stuff. They've lost touch with how we're doing on all sorts of measures, and without that, it's hard to focus on their work."

I was thrilled to see where they were going, but I didn't want to make it too easy for them. I guess a little of Martha's approach had rubbed off on me. I frowned, trying to pretend I wasn't getting it.

"Information, Will!" repeated Sheila. "Like the consultant said, it's not just about paying people more. Data is its own reward! We've got to give those guys information about how they're doing."

I kept stringing them along. "But we do that now. We have quarterly meetings with the entire Hyler staff. And we've got a newsletter."

Sheila shook her head. "Obviously, that doesn't cut it. The model you showed us says the most powerful way to affect behavior is immediate feedback, and we heard the same thing from the guys in the shop themselves. They need direct info on how their behavior is affecting things on a daily or even an hourly basis. That's the only way they'll know what kind of impact their actions are having."

"So what exactly are you proposing?" I asked. "Are we still taking out the impact posts?"

Luigi waved his hand. "Yes, of course. Work is starting on that in about twenty minutes. We've got to get rid of the obvious physical barriers to efficiency. But getting the data out there will have at least as much impact, we're pretty sure. We're going to start communicating exactly what's going on to the guys on the floor. Production stats, efficiency, safety information. With our basic systems, we've got all that data already. We've been talking to sales, and we think we can link things through there so we can also get the guys info on the orders that are made right through to the raw materials coming in."

I tried to look skeptical. "What makes you think this will work as a reinforcer?" I didn't say that their proposal was eerily similar to the example Martha had given me.

Sheila was starting to catch on to my ploy, but she indulged me anyway. "For one thing, the guys told us. For another, I've started doing a little reading on this stuff. Turns out we're not the first company to try out this approach to performance management. The Internet is a wonderful thing." She pointed to the jumble of papers on the desk in front of me. "I've got examples from several companies in there. One of the key elements in every behavior-based performance program I've been able to find out about is providing data as part of the cycle. So we're not exactly cutting-edge."

"It's hard to argue with the Internet. Because everything it says is true..." I trailed off and finally dropped my ruse. "I'm joking, I'm joking. I'm in. Let's get started."

Sheila started gathering up her papers. "We already have. We met with Amanda and the IT group this morning, and we've got a number of reporting initiatives underway."

I made a show of sighing. "I'm always the last to know."

Sheila smirked. "Don't be a drama queen. This was all your idea in the first place."

For some reason, I find people don't appreciate my dramatic nature in the way they should.

THIRTEEN

WILL APPLIES THE FRAMEWORK AT HOME

I RAISED MY glass of wine to toast my wife. "To more days like this one!"

Jenny raised her eyebrows at me. "Things go well today?" She sipped her own wine with less ceremony.

I nodded. "They did. The whole last week has been pretty good. At least I think so. We won't know for sure until we've had these new programs in place for a while and seen what happens with the results. But we're already seeing some behavior changes, and assuming we were right about which behaviors will give us the results we want, life should be sweet. We'll just have to stick with it now and reap the rewards." I was certainly hoping that would be the case. We'd invested quite a bit of time going down this particular road, and it wasn't as if we had any better ideas. I wasn't worried. Not at all. No, wait, I had it backward. I was completely worried. But then, that's what the wine was for. I took another sip.

My wife gave me a speculative look. "Now that you're a professional at this, why don't we take a moment to apply it to the home front?"

My worried feeling notched upward. "What did you have in mind?"

Jenny pursed her lips. "I've got lots of stuff in mind, mostly related to the kids."

"The kids? Those two little angels who float about our household spreading good cheer and happy dust? What possible application could this performance management stuff have for our lovely children?"

"Yes, hard to imagine, isn't it? But if the whole system of rewards and punishment and learning history and results is improving things at work, why wouldn't we try it at home?"

I shifted uncomfortably in my seat. "I don't know, honey. Wouldn't it seem as if we were training them like pets or something?"

"Oh, so it's OK to treat your work people like pets?" She shifted gears. "Anyway, when it comes right down to it, we are. And I have no issues with it. I don't think there's anything wrong with analyzing the situation around some of their behaviors and changing some things so that we *all* get the results we want."

I was still hesitant. Somehow it seemed different to apply this stuff to our kids, even though the intellectual part of my brain (small though it may be) was telling me the way the whole world runs could be explained by this framework. "How about an example?" I suggested. "What kind of behavior are we talking about? Is someone peeing on the carpet?"

Jenny laughed. "It's hard to start with just one. But yes, let's not try and change the world overnight. Let's start with some simple things that you don't see. Like your son."

"Our son," I corrected.

"He's your son in these discussions, Will. And you don't see a lot of these behaviors because I'm the one who looks after our kids most of the time. Like getting them up in the morning."

"OK," I said, unsure exactly whether she was saying it was my fault she was the primary caregiver. "What's the problem there?"

Jenny made an exasperated noise. "If you asked me what the most stressful thing is about my day, apart from hearing you talk about moving the family to Indonesia every night after work, it's nagging the kids out of bed every morning. You never see it, because you've already left for work by then."

"Seriously?" I asked. "It's that bad?"

"You have no idea, my dear."

"But they have alarm clocks," I said, puzzled. Well, they have phones that act like alarm clocks not to mention every other small household appliance. "How can this be an issue? They set their alarms, the alarm wakes them, they get up."

Jenny doesn't generally get mad enough to shout at me, but she's even scarier when she talks quietly. "I can't believe what I'm hearing, Will. I'm telling you, this is a problem. It's a problem for me. I don't sit here and tell you you're an idiot for paying your salespeople to sell products below cost and putting yourself out of business, do I? We all find ourselves in situations that aren't what we'd like, and I thought Martha's coaching was supposed to be applicable to all kinds of situations. Maybe what happens around here isn't *important* enough for you to think about?"

I wasn't so thick I couldn't work out the answer to that one. "ok, honey, I get it. I'm sorry for being an idiot. I'm overly focused on work these days, you're right." I took a deep breath and tried to look both thoughtful and confident. "Well, then. Let's start with what's going on now."

"ok," said Jenny.

"So, what's going on now?"

Jenny looked annoyed. "Not listening so well? I just explained that!"

I decided to paraphrase. "Well, you're saying the kids aren't getting up in the morning, despite having their own alarm clocks. But what happens exactly? They just lie in bed?"

"Yes," said Jenny. "Their alarms go off, but they either turn them off and go back to sleep or, in Jake's case, they sleep right through it. I'm downstairs in the kitchen, making breakfast and fuming, and finally I go upstairs and yell at them to get moving. Then I make a second trip, more nagging, maybe a third trip, and they finally get up. Then there's a mad rush for the bathroom, fighting because they both need to be in there at the same time, a scramble to eat breakfast, and then they run for the bus. Half the time, one of them misses it."

"So what happens then?" I asked.

Jenny blew some air out between her pursed lips. "I end up driving them to school, which makes me late for work."

"Honey," I interrupted, "you're a freelance writer. You work from home. How can you be late for work?"

"Will, as you well know, I treat working from home just like I'm going into an office. I want to be sitting at my desk, working, by 9:00 a.m.! When I end up driving the kids, I mess up my morning, and it frustrates the hell out of me. I have deadlines to meet and a household to run. In case you haven't noticed, I take care of all the errands, housekeeping, shopping, and cooking for the family. Plus I do writing assignments. I may not go to an office, but I still work!"

I held up my hands. "I'm sorry. I do get it. Anyway, it doesn't matter. What matters is we have a situation that isn't working and we need to change it. Let's apply the model. What's the result we want to get?"

Jenny thought about it for a minute. "Well, I want to get the kids out the door on time. And I don't want to be the big nag I always am. I want them to get themselves up and ready for school without me hounding them. I'm happy to make breakfast and get their lunches together, but I want them to get themselves out of bed and downstairs in time to eat and get out the door on time, so I don't have to drive them. And I don't want to own the whole process. I want *them* to take responsibility for it."

I nodded in what I hoped was a sympathetic manner. "OK, so that's where we want to get to. Let's look at what happens now." I went to the drawer beside the sink and pulled out a piece of paper and a pen. "If we're going to analyze this, let's do it right."

At that moment, Jake strolled into the kitchen. "Whatcha doing?" he asked.

I looked at Jenny. She shrugged. "Why shouldn't he hear this? It's not as if we're going to do anything he isn't going to know about."

Jake looked from me to his mother and back again. "How many glasses of wine have you guys had?"

I said, "Not that many, Jake. Have a seat. We're just applying some ideas that I've been using at work to some stuff here at home."

Jake looked suspicious. "What kind of stuff here at home?"

"The morning routine," I told him.

"Really? Do we have to?"

Jenny looked as if she might be about to throttle Jake, so I slapped the paper down in front of them and quickly sketched out:

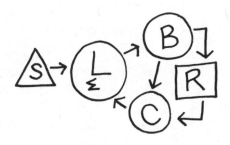

"What's that?" Jake asked.

I quickly walked him through the performance model, starting with "Result" and working backward. When I was done, he complained, "I'm not sure I like where this is going. That consequence thing sounds bad."

I said, "Don't worry about good or bad. Let's just look at what's going on in the mornings in terms of the model." I turned to Jenny. "What's the result we're getting now?"

"Apart from me getting old and gray and bitchy? The result is that I end up driving the kids to school half the time, and that messes up my day. And they don't take responsibility for themselves." She turned to Jake. "I really don't enjoy being the person who has to kick your butt to get you out the door in the morning."

Jake shrugged. "No argument there, Mom. I don't like it either."

Once again Jenny got an I'm-going-to-strangle-you look in her eyes, so I jumped in. "Good. Here's our starting point." I wrote:

Results:
- drive kids
- grumpy mom

The act of writing things down is supposed to help people clarify their thoughts, but it wasn't making Jenny feel any better. "'Grumpy mom'? That's how you describe it?" she demanded.

Jake, unaware of the dangerous ground we were treading, nodded vigorously. "Sounds right to me. I mean, Mom, you really do get grumpy. You nag me the whole way to school."

"Only because you miss your bus and I have to drive you, which messes up my day!"

"But, Mom," Jake started, "it's not like you w—"

"All righty!" I interrupted. "Let's carry on. Jenny, I'm just using that 'grumpy mom' description to summarize things. It's not a judgment. Moving backward through the model, let's look at the behavior. How would you describe that, honey? Now that Jake's here, he should hear it in your own words."

Jenny took a deep breath. "As I said, even though the kids have their own alarms, I still have to go in and wake them up, nag them out of bed, nag them downstairs, nag them to finish their breakfast, and nag them out the door so they can catch their bus. Somewhere in that process, about half the time one or both of them drags their butt just enough so I have to drive them to school."

I wrote down:

Behavior:
- sleep thru alarm
- dawdle getting ready
- miss bus

Jake said, "'Dawdle'? What's that?"

"To go slowly. As in 'dawdle along,'" I said.

"I don't know, Dad, is that a real thing? Did you just make that up?"

I sighed. "Don't make your own lack of vocabulary into one of those 'Wow, Dad, are you ever old and out of touch' conversations. Trust me, it's a word." I turned back to Jenny. "I know this isn't a comprehensive description, but let's go with it as a summary. Essentially the kids don't respond the way you'd like, starting with the alarm going off and ending with missing the bus. Even when they don't miss the bus, you have to nag them through the entire process. Is that fair?"

Jake answered before Jenny could. "Oh, that's fair, Dad. She goes nonstop until we're out the door. It's a little embarrassing, really."

I was amazed at how my son was failing to notice the danger signs of his imminent, and likely painful, demise. He started to say more, but I plowed on.

"Let's look at the consequences, then. We don't need too much discussion here, but it's important to think about them." I wrote:

Consequences:
- don't have to ride bus
- on time for school
- "not responsible"
Mom's day is messed up

"Here's an interesting thing," I pointed out. "Not only do the kids not have to ride the bus, but the bottom line is that they aren't late for school. Jake, what do you think about that?"

Jake looked at the list. "I guess that's all true, except I don't get the third one. What do you mean 'not responsible'? Are you saying it's not Mom's responsibility to get us to school on time?"

"Yes, that's part of the missing link, but let's come back to it. Let's start with the first one—how do you feel about riding the bus?"

Jake shrugged. "It's fine, I guess."

"Let me put it another way: Do you like riding the bus?"

Jake was more definitive. "No, nobody does. It stops, like, fifty times on the way to school, and there's all these boring people, and creepy people, all going to work who ride it. As soon as I can get my driver's license I'm never going near a bus again."

Jenny gave him a very skeptical stare. "You can't even get yourself out of bed in the morning. You think I'm going to trust you with a car?"

"Focus, people, focus!" I said. "So, Jake, riding the bus is not your favorite thing. What about being late for school? What happens then?"

"It sucks. You have to report to the principal's office and fill out a late slip, and then you get detention if you don't have a note. Plus, when you're late to class, you automatically get a special homework assignment. It totally sucks. There's no sympathy for kids being a little tired in the morning." Jenny's face made it clear she was in the "no sympathy" camp.

"So, Mom driving you means you don't have to ride the bus, *and* it means you avoid being late for school and all the stress that goes along with that. In other words, you're avoiding two somewhat unpleasant consequences. Is that a fair summary?"

Jake nodded.

Jenny said, "I see where this is going, Will, and I don't think it's going to help."

I held up my hand. "It was your idea to do this, honey, but I'm getting into it now, so let's follow it through. Next up is learning history."

"That's easy, " Jenny said. "The kids know I don't want them to be late for school. And if they're slow, they know I'll make sure they won't be late, starting with dragging them out of bed in the morning and finishing with driving them to school."

Jake chimed in. "And we appreciate it, Mom, we really do. You're a great mother."

Jenny glared at this obvious attempt at manipulation.

"ok, here's what the learning history looks like," I said, writing it down.

Learning History:
- Mom will make sure
I get to school on time

"It's more complicated than that, " I continued. "But there's the summary. In the end, the kids know you'll make sure they get to school on time. Sort of like that David Bowie song about modern love and the church..." I trailed off, waiting for public recognition of my clever reference to 1980s music.

Jake acted like he didn't even hear me.

"Whatever," I said. "So, the final piece. Again, from the kids' point of view, what's the stimulus that gets this whole thing rolling?"

Jenny said, "When the alarm goes off in the morning."

"Are you sure that's it?" I asked. I wrote down "alarm" along with something else:

Stimulus:
- alarm?
- nagging

"I'd say the alarm is actually *your* stimulus, honey," I pointed out. "When you hear the alarms blaring away and no one stirring, you go into their rooms and start the nagging cycle."

Jenny pursed her lips. "'Nagging cycle'? Is that a technical term? I don't remember Martha mentioning that one."

Jake looked surprised. "Martha as in G-squared Martha?" Instead of saying "great-grandmother," the kids had taken to calling her that. "What's she got to do with this?"

I ignored him. "ок, forget the 'cycle' part of it. But from the kids' perspective, this whole thing really starts when you come in to roust them out of bed, not when the alarm goes off."

Jenny looked at Jake. "Is that true? Is that why you're still lying there in bed when I come in to shut off the alarm?"

Jake looked a little uncomfortable. "Sort of...I guess. I mean, I need my sleep. Why would I get up before I absolutely have to? And it's great that you come in and...let me know when I definitely have to get up..."

Jenny did not look pleased about that, and I decided to continue treading lightly. "We may not like it, but it's important to map this situation out as it really happens so we can understand what's driving the whole thing. Right?

"Right," I answered myself. "So, to summarize: The stimulus is the alarm clock going off as well as the nagging. The alarm filters through the kids' learning history, which tells them that Mom will be coming in shortly to get them out of bed and that they can lie around until that point. In fact, it tells them that Mom will make sure they get to school somehow; that they don't have to worry about timing, because in the end, Mom will take care of it. The behavior is really a series of ass-dragging behaviors—"

"Dad!" Jake joked. "Language!"

"—a series of ass-dragging behaviors as they get ready to go to school. The result is that they miss the bus 50 percent of the time, and then Mom drives one or both of them to school. Mom is very grumpy about that, and her day is thrown off. The consequence for the kids is that they avoid the unpleasantness of riding the bus and they avoid the unpleasantness of being late for school."

"Hey," said Jake, "don't forget the other consequence. We have to ride in the car with Mom when she's super grumpy."

Jenny glared at him. "Oh, we can change that, Jake."

I decided to put a positive spin on things. "We can definitely change it. In fact, that's why we're having this discussion in the first place, right, honey?" I resisted the urge to point out this had been her idea in the first place. "Let's look at where we'd like to be. Jenny, how would you *like* the mornings to go?"

She got a dreamy look in her eyes. "What I'd really like is for the kids to take responsibility for getting themselves up, getting ready, eating breakfast, and getting out the door in time to catch the bus. So that I don't have to nag them, and I get down to work on time. *And* so I don't have to be the grumpy parent."

I looked at everything we'd written down. "This is obvious, but let's say it out loud anyway. What's happening right now, Jenny, is that you're reinforcing the kids for their current behavior. They know you're going to take care of them, so they're free to take their sweet time getting ready for school. Until you stop rewarding them for what they're doing, they'll keep doing it. Remember our conversation with Martha? What we need to employ here is what she called extinction."

"I know, you're right, Will. But there's one problem with this." Jenny looked a little embarrassed. "I'm a mom, Will, and you know what one of the primary drivers for a mother is?"

Jake piped up. "Getting to boss your kids around?"

My wife ignored him. "It's to keep your kids from harm. To keep them from experiencing pain. You want them to avoid getting hurt on the playground, or getting their hearts broken in a relationship, or failing a test. Anything like that."

I wasn't getting it. "So?"

"So, I don't want Jake and Sarah to miss the bus! I don't want them to get to school late, or to get in trouble and get detention. And I don't want the school calling me to ask why our kids can't get to school on time. I don't want any of that."

I was starting to feel uneasy about the model. Analyzing this situation made it clear that in real life there are interlocking patterns of reinforcement that can make a simple resolution difficult to achieve. I was staking a lot on Martha being right, though, so I pressed on regardless. "I get what you're saying, honey, but that puts up a roadblock, doesn't it? If you're not willing to let the kids suffer the consequences of their current behavior, I'm not sure we can change it. And I'm not sure you can keep complaining about it..."

Just then our daughter, Sarah, walked into the room. "What's going on?" she asked.

"Good thing you're here, Snot. Dad's trying to mess up our morning routine."

Nice, eh? My son's pet name for his sister is "Snot." It's not quite as bad as it sounds. When they were both very little, and Jake was just learning to speak, he couldn't quite say "Sarah," so he said "Snot." The nickname has never quite gone away, and Sarah doesn't even notice it anymore.

"That's not exactly what's happening," I said. I gave Sarah a quick backgrounder on our discussion.

"I'm with Jake," she said after I finished. "Mom, I get why you're so grumpy, but I don't want to be late for school. And I'm not keen on that creepy bus either."

I replied before Jenny did. "But don't you think it's unfair to put your mother in the position of having to be the grumpy one, just so you can get to school? You guys are taking no responsibility for yourselves. And until you feel the pain of being late for school, I don't see that changing." I was getting angry, I realized, and letting myself fall into another interlocking pattern of reinforcement: when I'm mad, I want to punish. Like many people of my generation, I had been raised to suffer the consequences of my actions. Part of that pattern was doing things to avoid punishment, rather than doing things to be rewarded. If it was good enough for my dad, why couldn't it work for my kids?

Jenny must have been thinking along the same lines. "Why does there have to be a negative outcome in this for the kids to change?"

"Because sometimes a smack upside the head is a good teaching tool," I said. "Metaphorically speaking."

"But, Will, I thought the most powerful way to influence behavior was immediate, positive rewards. Isn't using punishment an issue? Or using the threat of punishment? Aren't those supposed to be less effective?"

I was feeling defensive. "Martha never said anything about *not* using punishment. She just said it wasn't the best way to achieve the results you want in the long term."

"Exactly," Jenny said. "And yet what we're talking about here really *is* the long term. This is every day before school for the next four years, and then the kids will be out on their own at college or university. This is a lesson for the rest of their lives. So is punishment really the way to go here?"

I exhaled heavily. "Maybe that's called life, Jenny. Half the things we do are to avoid unpleasant consequences. It's not about a bell ringing and chocolates falling from the sky every time we do something right. Sometimes we do stuff to keep bad things from happening."

Sarah said, "But, Dad, I think you like the stuff you do for that reason."

I stared at her. "Huh?"

"I think you find that kind of stuff rewarding. You like putting snow tires on the car in the fall so you don't get caught in the snow without them. You like getting to the airport early to make sure you don't miss your flight. You're not doing those things because you're scared of the bad stuff—you feel good about them."

"So what?"

Sarah gestured with what almost looked like enthusiasm. "Don't you get it? You keep doing that stuff because it's rewarding, *not* punishing. I don't think you're even doing it to avoid punishment. It's like what you told us G-squared said. Rewards have the best long-term effects on behavior."

"You're right, Snot," said Jake. "Dad's a total old man that way. His biggest thrill in life is avoiding having anything unexpected happen. It's like his dream day if it can all be super planned out and totally boring."

"Hey," I said. "Why is that boring?"

"We can talk about this later, Will," said Jenny. She seemed amused for some reason. "I think the kids have a point here. If you think about most things you do, that we all do, we do them because we find them rewarding. Maybe we start doing something because of the fear of punishment, but eventually, if we keep doing it, we're getting some kind of reward from that."

"I don't get any joy from filling the car up with gas," I protested. "I do it because running out of gas is very inconvenient."

"Some things we do are to avoid bad things, sure," Jenny conceded. "But if we want to make something a habit, why wouldn't we try to set it up so it was rewarding and not just punishment avoidance?"

"Well, uh, I don't know," I stammered. "Maybe because we've only got so much energy to go around? And setting life up so that buzzers go off and money falls from the sky isn't always practical?"

Sarah said, "Dad, you're, like, being a total stick in the mud. Let's see where Mom's going with this."

Jenny smiled at Sarah. "Thank you, honey. I appreciate the support. Perhaps certain other members of the family could learn from your positive attitude."

"Standing right here, Jenny," I said.

She ignored me and addressed the kids. "Although part of me would get a certain satisfaction from it, a bigger part of me doesn't want you two to suffer for being lazy-asses in the morning. I guess if I just stopped being your alarm clock on top of your actual alarm clock, and stopped being the bus to school, you'd eventually figure it out."

I nodded emphatically. "In about two days, Jenny. Believe me, you would find it satisfying to watch."

My wife carried on. "But I wonder if there's another alternative, some kind of compromise that results in you getting yourselves up and to school without me nagging you, and without it ruining the start to my workday."

Jenny looked at both our kids. "Instead of setting up a pattern where you're avoiding punishment, how do we set it up so that you get rewarded for getting yourselves going in the morning?" I was feeling like a complete outsider at this point, even though I was supposed to be the expert.

Jake suggested, "How about we don't have to go to school at all? You, like, homeschool us?"

Sarah made an exasperated noise, looking almost scarily like her mother. "Moron. That's a stupid idea. What about sports? And your friends? We're not solving the problem of whether we have to go to school." She turned to look at her mother. "If I'm honest with myself, I think the bus ride is the thing I don't like. And knowing that you're able to drive me if I miss it, well, maybe that affects me when I'm getting going in the morning."

"Of course it does," I jumped in. "You can't help yourself, because the consequence you get for being late is that you avoid an unpleasant experience. Or you replace it with an experience that's more fun. Who wouldn't want to be chauffeured to school? Hell, honey, how about I sleep in a little and you can drive me to work?" I paused for a bit of emphasis. "So long as you reward dragging their butts with driving, it'll keep happening."

Jenny looked thoughtful. "What about you, Jake, is riding the bus your biggest issue?"

Jake shrugged. "Like I already said, who likes riding a city bus? None of my friends are on it, plus it takes twice as long as when you drive."

Jenny said, "What if we turned our thinking on its head a little? You guys like the drive to school. What if that was the reward for getting yourselves going in the morning? What if you were ready to go on time, you'd get a ride to school? But if you're not, you find your own way to school. You catch a later bus and be late?"

"But, honey," I sputtered in what was almost certainly a highly unattractive way (I mean, who looks good sputtering?), "I thought one of the major problems was you starting your workday late because you have to drive the kids to school at the last minute?"

Jenny looked at the kids. "Working from home can be very challenging for me. There are always errands to run, stuff to clean, all that sort of thing. I find to make it work I have to be very disciplined about my hours of work, and that means starting no later than 9:00 a.m. But if we left the house at 8:00 a.m., I'd have plenty of time to drive you and be back home to start work before 9:00 a.m."

I scoffed. Inside I was asking myself how I'd become the skeptic in this whole process, but in my outside voice I said, "Seriously? They can't be ready for 8:25 a.m. to get out the door for the bus with you nagging them the whole way. You think they can suddenly be ready at 8:00 a.m.?"

"It doesn't really matter what I think." She turned back to the kids. "What do you guys think?"

Sarah was looking very enthusiastic. "To get a ride every day? I could totally do that!"

Jake seemed keen as well. "Yeah, Mom, I could commit to that."

"But there's a catch to this," Jenny told them. "I'm not the one doing all the driving."

Uh-oh, I thought, this isn't looking good for me. I jumped in. "Honey, I can't hang around the house to be a chauffeur. You know how crazy work is right now—"

Jenny held up her hand. "That's not what I'm talking about, Will." She turned back to Sarah and Jake. "We aren't the only family with this problem. There's a reason you don't see your friends on the bus. I've been talking to a bunch of the other moms and dads at the school, and it turns out that a lot of kids are getting driven to school." Suddenly I had the feeling that Jenny had planned where this was going right from the start. "It turns out there is a lot of interest in carpooling. The Turchanskys, the Besters, and the Glyckherrs all have kids at the high school, they all have problems getting their kids to school, and most importantly, they all have seven-passenger vehicles."

Jake looked slightly less enthusiastic. He said, "But Darren Turchansky's a bit of a geek."

Sarah knew a good deal when she saw one. "Who cares? You're a bit of a geek." She turned to Jenny. "I'd way rather carpool than ride that stinky bus. Jake would too, he just hasn't realized it yet. Even if it means we have to get up earlier."

Jenny said sternly, "But this arrangement has no flexibility for people to be late. When we agree on the pickup time, there's no negotiating. It won't matter who's driving, if you're not ready to go when it's time, you're finding your own way to school."

"And you won't feel guilty about that?" I asked Jenny. "Because I guarantee you there will be some days when one of them isn't ready."

Jenny shrugged. "Not as much. I'm making an effort to help them, and anyway, if they miss the car, they still have time to catch the bus. So they're not automatically late."

I kept pushing. "And you don't mind driving them?"

Jenny shook her head. "I wouldn't feel good about driving them every day. That's a lot of time, and it feels a bit wasteful. But I have to admit that one of the things about driving, even when I'm grumpy, is that I get a little time with them. It's those interlocking patterns of behavior and reinforcement you were talking about. Sure, I'm grumpy about starting my workday late, but getting to spend a little extra time with them once or twice a week is a reward."

"ok," Jake said, "but you can't talk about weird family stuff when we've got all those other kids in the car. I still gotta go to school with them."

Jenny smiled. "Don't worry, Jake, I won't embarrass you. Besides, it's only a fifteen-minute drive. You can probably survive anything for that long."

Jake shrugged. "ok, whatever."

The conversation continued, and details were worked out about what time alarms needed to be set for and about what Jenny wouldn't do to get them going, as well as what she would. In about fifteen minutes they had a plan worked out, and then the kids disappeared again into the electronic abyss, happy to use up their remaining screen time before the mandatory dark period before bedtime.

After they ran upstairs, Jenny came over to give me a big hug and a kiss. "Thanks, Will," she said.

"For what?"

"For walking me through that process. I really think Martha is onto something in terms of understanding the scorpion's nature. We all do what we get rewarded for, and those rewards can come from outside or inside. It's a revelation to realize that I got rewarded in some way by the kids' bad behavior. It's hard to see it when you're in the situation, and it's even harder to admit it." She gave my hand a squeeze. "And I appreciate you playing devil's advocate, too. I think it would be hard to figure this stuff out if you didn't have someone pushing back." She leaned in and gave me another kiss, this one lasting a little longer. "Maybe we should head upstairs, too. There might be a good five-minute window between when the kids go to bed and when I stop feeling like having more of this."

As I tried not to trip over my feet rushing up the stairs behind her, I decided not to spoil the moment by voicing my suspicion that she'd planned the whole conversation, and that I was just her puppet in the process. I figured I'd let both of us pretend that I had some wisdom for a while before disabusing her of that notion.

FOURTEEN

MARTHA RUMINATES ON IMPLEMENTING THE PERFORMANCE PRINCIPLE

I TOOK ANOTHER long drag on my pipe and paid for it only mildly, with a few hacking coughs. It was well worth it.

"Well, Willie, it sounds like you're on track now and doing a few things right. Question is, will it be enough? Are the numbers going to show the results as quickly as you need them?"

He gave me a sardonic look. "What? I thought success was guaranteed if I followed your advice."

I chuckled. "You know by now there are only two guarantees in life."

"Death and taxes?" he asked.

"That works," I said. "But I was going to say 'happiness' and 'sadness.' It remains to be seen which one you're going to experience."

He shrugged. "It's all about the timing, isn't it? There's no question we're doing the right things. As you say, though, it's a question of whether we'll see good enough results before Ralph pulls the plug. I kind of get the feeling he's looking for an excuse to close us down."

I raised my eyebrows. "I haven't heard you say that before." I blew a smoke ring that floated out off the porch and caught the evening breeze.

Will nodded. "Yeah, I've been using my spare time when not worrying about patterns of reinforcement to worry about that. I've been thinking about all the acquisitions Mantec has made in the last few years, and all the stuff we've gotten rid of. I'm just not sure Hyler fits with the company's strategy anymore."

Now it was my turn to shrug. "Not much you can do about that, Willie. Like they say, there are two things you really shouldn't worry about: what you can change and what you can't." I could guess what he was thinking: the old girl is certainly full of useless wisdom tonight. Sometimes it's fun to spout platitudes at people. You can't really argue with 'em, because they're true, but that doesn't make them any less useless. "But seriously, Willie, there *isn't* much you can do about that. Whether Mantec really wants to get out of Hyler or not, the best thing you can do is make sure the business is running as well as it can."

"Yeah, yeah, I know that. Maybe I'm speculating wildly about things like getting sold off because I don't have enough anxiety in my life. I mean, how could I possibly get out of bed without anxiety to drive me?" He looked at me. "You want a beer to go with that nasty pipe?"

I chuckled. "I like the way you think, young man."

Once Will had returned and I had cracked open the bottle, I prompted him for more. "So, what kind of results are you getting so far? It's been two months now since you changed your sales team's incentive plan and you changed processes and safety on the manufacturing floor. What are you seeing?"

Will grinned. "Despite the union's bitching, we haven't seen any change in the number of accidents. Well, actually, that's not true. The accident rate is *down* because we're seeing fewer collisions on the shop floor between forklifts and impact posts. And we're seeing significantly more efficiency in the manufacturing process. Actually, what we're *seeing* is information. And lots of it."

I wasn't surprised, but I wanted to hear him explain it. "What do you mean, Willie?"

He said, "We're getting information about production rates, efficiency by machine, wait time for inventory, inventory buildup, parts and supplies inventory information: all sorts of details about the production process. Remember how we talked about what people find rewarding, and you said it's not just money or more holidays? You mentioned information as a reward. We started a scoreboard of basic production information, including safety, and it's escalated. We almost can't keep up with all the data. We're giving the production guys feedback on how they're doing almost hourly now, and they're turning that into a competition to see how they can do things even more efficiently. The weird thing is that it was like flipping a switch. As soon as we started doing this, our results started changing."

I wagged my pipe back and forth in front of him. "Not exactly, Willie. Once the behavior of your people changed, *then* your results changed. Don't forget what drives results."

"Yeah, exactly," Will agreed. "Of course. And the behaviors didn't change until we changed the whole pattern of reinforcement. Once we started rewarding different behavior, we started getting different behavior."

"Funny how that works, isn't it?" I took a drink of beer and then a deep draw on my pipe. Life can be wonderful with alcohol and tobacco. Just not necessarily long. But even that doesn't always work out.

Will stood up and started pacing. He seemed to do that a lot when he was thinking. "I was actually more worried about the sales team. Production seemed more controlled to me, more quantifiable. You make this change, you can get this result. But sales, well, those folks are dealing with market demand and all the fuzziness that goes along with it. You can't make people buy something if they don't want it. You could have a great commission structure on selling dog poop, but if the market doesn't want dog poop, it won't make a difference. Plus, the sales team have really been our information source about what's going on out there. They weren't keen on the change, they said, because it wasn't in line with what the market wanted." Will paused. "But I guess we just have to chalk this one up to the nature versus nurture debate." I looked at him quizzically, although I was pretty sure I knew what he meant. "You know, the one where we debate whether our kids are the way they are because of some set of innate personality characteristics, or whether it's their environment that shapes them. And the answer is always: who knows? When you think about it, it's probably both."

I smiled. "I take it you're seeing a change in sales?"

Will nodded. "It's killing me to think about how long we kept that old incentive scheme in place." He started pacing again. "Almost immediately, we saw the sales numbers on the profitable products shoot straight up. All that talk about what the market wanted? All that worry about our sales going to zero because people didn't want products that we made actual money on? Poof, all gone."

I decided to probe a little, to ensure he was seeing the whole picture. "Did your sales mix change very much? Or did the deals the salespeople were making change?"

Will seemed to be expecting the question. "Yeah, that's what I was wondering about. What I thought would happen didn't happen. Our sales guys did a bit of both. They started moving some of the more profitable stuff they hadn't done much with before, but they also stopped dropping their pants on pricing for the stuff they were already selling lots of. With the improvements to the production process, they can promise ridiculously fast delivery times, and we can make that happen without getting killed on penalties for failing to meet the timing. The really unexpected thing is that the average salesperson is going to make *more* in commissions if the situation keeps up like this."

I nodded wisely, as if that was exactly what I had expected. Because that *was* exactly what I had expected. "It's interesting how those things happen, isn't it? Market forces absolutely play a role in all of this, but we influence market forces much more than we realize."

"Yeah, I guess we do," Will said. "Our overall sales volume hasn't changed a whole lot, but our product mix has shifted a bit, and our pricing has gone up. We're driving more revenue on that volume, and with our production efficiency, we're spending less to produce that volume too. Bottom line is that there *is* a bottom line. Even if we don't grow the sales side dramatically, at least we're making money in the here and now, and we can start exploring more new products, spending money on R & D, and all that good stuff."

I took another sip of beer and belched loudly. Will laughed out loud. "What's so funny?" I asked him.

He shook his head. "It's the image of you...never mind. It doesn't matter."

I kept my amusement to myself. "So why are you worried about how Mantec is going to react to all of this if things are going so well?"

Will sat back down on the swing. "Because I worry. That's what I do. That and the fact that I've got a call with Ralph on Monday to go over all the numbers, which I won't have in my hands until Friday." He pushed off with his legs and swung back and forth. "Did I tell you we're now tackling Hyler's performance review system?"

"Really?" I said. "I thought that's what you'd been doing all along."

"Yeah, ha ha. I mean the one for the supervisors, the administrative staff, the whole management team. You know how most organizations have this lame process where people complete a performance review form on their team members once a year, which generally has no impact on the person's day-to-day behavior, development, or anything else? That's what I mean."

"I'm impressed," I said. "That's very ambitious of you. Most organizations don't drive the Performance Principle that far into the organization."

Will looked at me. "The Performance Principle? Did you just verbally capitalize that?"

"Good catch, Willie. That's what I call this behavioral framework. There are other names for it, but Bill and I coined the term along with some help from our friend Burrhus. Burrhus had a more precise and scientific name for the process, but Bill and I wanted everyone to be able to relate to it and not be intimidated. Think we should trademark it?"

"Why not?" Will said. "Do you mind if I borrow it in the meantime, royalty-free?"

I waved my pipe at him magnanimously. "Go ahead. But tell me more about what you're doing with your performance review process."

Will got a strange smile on his face. "Funny how word gets around about things. In the beginning, everybody was scared of what we were doing with the sales group. Everybody was worried that Will was doing all this weird stuff just to get the place shut down. A few months later, every department wants to talk about behaviors and results and rewards. Even the HR folks.

"I can't remember how much I told you about Mark Goldman's feelings about all this, but he was one of the early resisters. He kept saying things like, 'This is that crazy behavior-modification, mind-control stuff that was popular for a while in the '50s.' He kept calling me the Manchurian candidate and saying that it wasn't ethical to control people's behavior."

"And how did that make you feel, Willie?" I asked him.

"What are you, my shrink now? His comments were silly, but they made me realize you need to be careful in explaining to people how this process works, because clearly he didn't understand what we had been doing. His objection to the process seemed to come from the idea that there's some way to make people do something they don't want to do." Will laughed. "If we could do that, then we'd *really* have something. Anyway, it took a while with Mark. I had to get him to see that there's nothing evil or mind-control-like about this process. When he finally got it, he really got it. The place he wanted to apply it was our internal performance review system.

Once Mark saw what had happened with the sales people and out on the production floor, he decided he wanted to make all that good stuff happen with the staff and the management team."

"You look skeptical," I said. "You don't believe the Performance Principle can work in that kind of situation?"

Will shook his head. "No, it's not that. It's just that in my work with Mantec over the years, I've seen the performance review process in what must be all of its worst forms. At our software division down in Emeryville, they had what I consider to be the greatest example I've ever seen of the process gone wrong—even worse than how things were here when I arrived. I got involved there because Lean Six Sigma was working so well in other areas of the company they figured maybe it could help with performance review too. They had evolved the process in the weirdest way. Ironically, it was all in an attempt to make the process better and improve performance."

I took a long drag on my pipe. "They always start that way, Willie, my boy. And they don't always pay attention to how the world actually works. What did you find in Emeryville?"

"Well, for starters, they decided every employee should receive a ranking that summarized their performance. The scale was a simple 1 to 10, where 10 meant you were a super-fantastic employee and 1 meant you sucked. They went merrily along until the VP of HR noticed that everyone was getting ranked as 7 or higher. Based on her memory of her college statistics course, she figured that couldn't be true. In reality, any given sample of employees should show a distribution of rankings that looks somewhat like a bell curve, with most of the group clustered around the middle and a couple of outliers at each end. To her, the company's results meant that the evaluators were being too nice and not objective enough.

So she solved the problem by decreeing that every department could rate only a certain percentage of employees higher than 7, and that every department also had to rate a certain percentage below 3. She was basically saying that the performance managers were biased, that they didn't want to give out low scores, and that no group of people could be that good. Which, by the way, I would agree with on paper. Her new directive caused great consternation and confusion, particularly because salary increases and promotions were tied to employee ratings. It's not that you could necessarily fault her logic; it's just that her decree had wildly unintended consequences—"

"Let me guess," I interrupted him. "Among other things, you probably had supervisors negotiating with other supervisors to trade both good and bad scores."

I felt smug when Will looked surprised. "'Of course. Why wouldn't you have a good idea of what would happen?" he conceded. "Yes, among other things, the supervisors got into horse trading to protect 'good' employees they couldn't give a 7 or higher to, because they'd used up their 7's, and the same thing happened with employees who really weren't that bad but were the top candidates to score under 3. There was also significant lying about performance in order to get some of the lower-scoring employees out of one supervisor's area and into someone else's. The end result was that the group spent a huge percentage of its time worrying about, fiddling with, and messing up the whole performance review system. Productivity for the company was in the toilet, employee morale was brutally low, and when I walked in there it was as if I had joined the late stages of *Survivor*..."

I gave him a blank look.

"Uh, how about *The Apprentice*?" he asked me.

"Nope. But I'm guessing those are what they call reality TV shows, where people are initially formed into teams but then are pitted against each other because there can be only one winner? And the theoretical attraction is that there is a whole pile of drama while they lie to each other as they're waiting for the first chance to stab each other in the back?"

"Wow," Will explained. "You're telling me you've never seen one of those shows?"

"No, but I've heard about them. Their premise is not new. I've always found it amazing that people want to create drama in their workplace. I find it even more amazing that people would want to waste their spare time on it."

Will laughed. "I hear you. Particularly about the work side of things. The workplace should be a no-drama zone. But the challenge is, if you're not analyzing the situation in order to understand the interlocking patterns of behavior and reinforcement, you can keep making things worse instead of better."

I blew a smoke ring at him. "And people usually do. Ever heard the expression 'The road to hell is paved with good intentions'? What you're describing isn't the standard interpretation of it, but you see it all the time in the workplace, in the home, and in relationships in general. We don't always know why people do what they do, and as you and I have discussed, we frequently assume that what we find rewarding will be rewarding in the same measure to everyone else. To top it off, we don't always take the time to figure out what behaviors will give us the results we want!" I noticed I was talking loudly and was a bit out of breath. "Sorry, Willie, but I get excited about this. The world likes to believe in concepts like 'attitude' and 'unselfishness,' when really, thinking that way can make things much worse." I took a swig of my beer, emptying it. I waggled the bottle in front of Will's face. "I need to calm down, Willie. Beer me."

When he returned with two more, I asked him to continue his story. "The problems I saw in Mantec's Emeryville division were dramatic, but back then I didn't have a useful perspective or mental framework to help me understand or address the issues. We did improve things somewhat. We held a bunch of facilitated workshops, and the performance review process was revealed as the culprit in a hurry. We ended up ditching it and going back to the regular Mantec process which at best was benign, and at worst was a complete waste of time.

"At Hyler, our current performance review system is similar, but it was never implemented to that extreme. It didn't create the same level of drama, for the most part, but it didn't create any improvement either. But kudos to Mark. Once he saw good things happening elsewhere, he changed his tune and wanted to dive full-on into using the Performance Principle."

"Five cents, please, Willie," I said. "Royalty payments start now."

Will smiled. "Put it on my tab."

"How are you tackling this, then?" I asked him.

Will took a sip of his beer. "Very simplistically. And slowly. The problem we're running into with a lot of the staff jobs—which is to say, everyone who isn't actually selling our products or hands-on making them—is that it's hard to quantify the results we need and the behaviors that produce them down to the individual level."

"Well, Willie, why don't you just fire everyone and then see if anything goes wrong? Saves you money in the short term, and you can always hire back the people you need." I belched again. He ignored me. The belching, at least.

"Don't think we haven't talked about that," he continued. "If you can't define a result that a particular person contributes to, well, then, what value are they really adding? This goes directly back to my Lean training. In Lean—"

I interrupted to keep the story going. I was starting to worry about whether I'd live to the end of it. "Yes, yes. In the Lean philosophy, all activities that don't create value for the customer are considered waste and need to be eliminated from the process. I am passing familiar with it, Willie. I spent time in Japan at Toyota after the war. Or had you forgotten that?" I was rewarded by a sour look. Why I take pleasure in pissing people off in small ways is really beyond me.

"Anyway," Will said, "we started to focus in on defining the result we needed from each of the staff jobs. We've worked through about twenty jobs so far. We're applying Lean to understand the results and the behaviors we need to get them, and then we'll apply the Performance Principle, trademarked by Martha the Magnificent, to align the reward structure with the behaviors. For the accounts payable and accounts receivable staff, we have some specific metrics around processing times and error rates. For Mark, as the HR lead, it was more difficult to quantify, but he insisted we do his job early on. He felt it would add credibility if the rest of the staff saw him going through the process personally. Not that they needed much convincing after watching the sales and production people.

"When we drilled into it, the results we needed from Mark were fuzzy, but not indefinable. We wanted to improve morale at Hyler and maintain it at a certain level. We wanted to keep retention at a certain level too. We went out on a limb and also established some goals for implementing and maintaining the new performance review process, which we haven't really finished inventing.

Then we did some detailed planning on what Mark would need to do to achieve each of those goals. We broke it down into what he needs to be doing weekly and monthly. After that, we figured out how we would track it, and then we talked about rewards. And you know what feedback we're getting about rewards?"

I made a very educated guess. "So far, people are so excited about being able to measure their own progress they figure that's all the reward they need."

Will chuckled. "Right again. I'm not sure it will stay that way forever, but initially it's like with the production guys—people are jazzed about knowing what they need to do to contribute, and getting regular feedback about that is satisfying to them. We mapped all of this out into a format that Mark coined a name for: MAPP. Can you hear the capitalization? And the two 'P's? It stands for Measurable, Achievable Performance Plan."

I rolled my eyes. "If I had a nickel for every stupid acronym..."

"Yes," Will agreed, "but people like acronyms, so if that's what it takes to keep them interested, I'm fine with it. Don't forget, Martha, we don't all find the same things reinforcing." I blew him a raspberry. He was unfazed. "We're getting people to document items in their own MAPPs, and we've changed the review schedule. Instead of reviews being done annually, we're going to start having managers meet every two weeks with their team members."

I decided to play devil's advocate. "Won't that suck up a lot of time that people could be using to work?"

Willie didn't bite. "Ha ha. I see what you're doing here. But to complete my lesson as a dutiful student, the answer is yes, it will take time. However, as a brilliant consultant explained to me, changing behavior will be most successful when rewards are delivered as quickly as possible. The plan is for these biweekly meetings to be short. Since they're based on reviewing quantifiable measures and results, there's no need for long, qualitative discussions. But it's early days yet."

I persisted with my questioning. "What about the tough-to-quantify things that you want people to develop and exercise? Like leadership? Or collaboration?"

Will furrowed his brow. "Yeah, well, like I said, we're still in early days here. I think I can see where you're going, and no, I haven't done a MAPP for myself yet. It's actually something I wanted to talk to you about, because I haven't got my head around it yet."

"Oh, that's a good topic, Willie, my boy. And a conversation we'll definitely need to have. We'll want to cover what I like to call 'summary words': words that pack a whole bunch of meaning but mean different things to different people. We already mentioned 'attitude,' and there are more." I knocked my pipe out against the side of my rocker. "But that's going to have to wait until next time, Willie. This old gal is tuckered out." I heaved myself to my feet, waving off Will's offered hand. "I ain't dead yet, Willie. I can still stand up on my own. Talk to me when I turn 105, though. I may need some help then." I shuffled over to the screen door and stopped on the sill. "Or if you force me to drink more than two beers. For now, it seems to me you need to stay the course and see if the results follow."

I felt bad when I saw the anxious look on his face. "But what do you think, Martha? Overall, are we on the right track?"

I'm way too old and experienced in the quirkiness of life to be able to claim anything is certain. Like Will said, if Hyler's performance turned around but Mantec wanted to divest, it wouldn't matter. If his boss was convinced that offshoring was the right thing to do despite the plant's performance, it also wouldn't matter. If there was a glitch in their accounting system at month-end because a moth crawled into their server room and ate the hard drive, everything could all come crashing down. In life, whether you're doing the right thing or not, there are never any guarantees. But Will wasn't asking me about life; he was looking for reassurance. Although I like to tease him, there's a difference between that kind of fun and being just plain mean. I wasn't nearly old enough for that. "Will, I think you're on exactly the right track." I said.

FIFTEEN

WILL HAS A SURPRISE VISITOR

IT DIDN'T MAKE any rational sense, but when I got home that night, I was feeling more anxious than when I'd arrived at Hyler a little more than six months before. My latest conversation with Martha had had the effect of both making my intellectual self feel better and making my emotional self feel worse.

Which was probably why I'd missed whatever was going on with Jenny.

"You don't even know what's different, do you?" she asked me.

I don't know about you, but I've always hated the game of guess-what-your-spouse-has-done-differently-to-his/her-hair/clothes/makeup/emotional-self. If I haven't noticed a change in the first eight seconds, I am generally not going to without some assistance.

This time, however, Jenny didn't seem bothered by me missing it. "C'mon, honey," she prompted. "Surely you can notice it?"

I slumped down on the sofa. "Sorry, babe, but my antennae are in sleep mode or something. All of this work stress is distracting me."

She smiled. "I know, Will, but this is something that should make your work stress better."

I looked at her more closely. "I'm really not seeing it."

She laughed. "What you see, my dear, is a less grumpy wife! How can you miss that?"

That was a question in the same category as "Does this make me look fat?" There was no safe way to answer. "What are you talking about, Jenny, and what does it have to do with my work?"

Jenny sat down on the sofa next to me. "Well, everything and nothing, Will, but it should make you feel better regardless. Do you know what today is the one-month anniversary of?"

I shook my head. "Some relationship milestone Sarah's reached with some almost-boyfriend that is going to make *me* grumpy?" Visions of Blaine jumped into my head.

"No, no, honey. Not that. It's been a full month since we had our intervention with the kids."

I managed to recall the conversation. Had it been a month already? It seemed like just a few days ago. "Great," I said. "I hope. How's it going?" You'd think I would have known the answer to that, living in the same house as Jenny and the kids, but I'd been so focused on work I had lost touch.

Jenny kept smiling. "It's going extremely well, Will. In fact, it's nothing short of a miracle."

"A miracle? Really? I could use a miracle right about now."

She continued. "Remember way back when the kids were just babies, and we were at our wits' end over their sleep patterns? And then we followed that simple program and suddenly they were sleeping through the night on their own?"

"Yes, I remember it well."

"Well, this ranks up there with that experience. Amazing!"

I found myself smiling too. "So you're saying our analysis worked? The kids changed their behavior around getting up and going to school?"

Jenny nodded vigorously. "Actually, we all changed our behavior around the morning routine. I got the carpool going and stopped nagging. The kids changed literally overnight and started getting their asses in gear in time to get driven. I became less grumpy; now I'm just a carpool chauffeur who gets occasional extra quality time with her kids. And the kids are now taking full responsibility for getting themselves out of bed and ready for school."

I felt a skeptical look creep across my face. "Overnight? Our kids? Changed? And here's the big one: taking *responsibility*? Are you sure, honey? Are you saying they've done it every day?"

"I know, I know, it sounds impossible. And it hasn't been perfect. The second week in, Jake didn't hear his alarm, slept in, missed the drive, and had to take the bus. I'll tell ya, it was the second-hardest thing in the world not to go shake him. The hardest was not driving him, particularly because it wasn't my day to drive in the pool. I could easily have driven him on his own. But I didn't. And the weird thing is, he never said anything about it. He didn't come whining to me after school, and I hardly felt guilty at all. Well, I did feel guilty, but I got over it. And that was the only time—"

At that moment Sarah walked into the living room. "The only time what?" she interrupted.

"Your mother was just explaining how getting out of the house in the morning is working much better."

Sarah shrugged. "Yeah, it's good."

"Good?" I said. "It sounds amazing!"

Sarah cocked her head and thought for a moment. "Well, no, not really, Dad. It just makes sense. Mom put us on our own for getting up, but she gave us an incentive to do it. It's not that hard."

Jenny looked at me. "See? Not that hard. We figured out what result we wanted, what behavior we needed to get the result, how to reward that behavior, and of course it changed. It's how people work, Will. It's the scorpion's nature."

"Don't forget we also took away the reinforcement for the behavior you didn't want," I said, sounding almost as if I knew what I was talking about. "We didn't only reward the new behavior, we stopped rewarding the old."

Sarah was busily texting on her phone by this point. "Whatever, parents."

I gave Jenny a look. "So I guess that means I should reward you with a little naughty behavior, eh, honey?"

"Dad, gross!" my daughter said.

Jenny smirked. "Remember that whole thing about not assuming what you find rewarding is rewarding for everyone else?"

I laughed.

"NICE OF YOU to roll in," Ralph said.

I started and almost dropped my coffee. There, sitting in my chair in my office, was Ralph Borsellino, CEO of Mantec, and the man I most wanted to not see.

"Jesus, Ralph, you scared me. What the hell are you doing here?"

Ralph had been flipping through some papers on my desk. He stood up. "We have a meeting."

"Yeah," I agreed, "on the phone, Ralph. On the phone. And your phone is in Chicago. What are you doing here in person?" As I said the words, I got a sinking feeling in my stomach. I didn't want to know the answer to that question.

It must have shown on my face. "This is why you're a terrible poker player, Will. You wear your heart on your sleeve." He walked around the desk and stood in front of me. "Got a meeting room we can go sit in?"

I put my laptop down on my desk. "Look, why don't you just give me the bad news right here?"

Ralph looked amused. "You're such a pessimist, Will. But I didn't fly all the way out here to sit in your cramped office—let's find some space. Really, as the president of the company, I think you could stand to have a slightly bigger office."

"You know me: always trying to save the company a buck." I headed out the door for the conference room.

"More likely you were too nice to kick someone out of a decent office," Ralph said. Which was actually true; I'd grabbed one of the spare offices when I showed up back at Hyler. It was not the most luxurious, but I'd stopped noticing after the second day.

A few moments later we slid into leather chairs across from each other in the conference room. "Now, that's a little better, isn't it?"

My experience with Ralph is that when he asks a question, he already knows how he wants you to answer it. I nodded. "Let's cut to the chase, Ralph."

"What? No pleasantries? No 'How are you doing, Ralph? How's life at corporate?'"

"We talk every few weeks, Ralph. I know how life is at corporate. Besides, since when have you been about pleasantries?" I leaned back in my chair. "Anyway, I think you're making a mistake by closing Hyler down. Just look at the numbers we've put up in the last three months. Our sales are up, our profitability is way up because of all the efficiencies we've implemented, and morale at the plant is dramatically better than when I arrived."

"You're not officially in the black on a monthly basis yet," Ralph pointed out.

"No," I said, exasperated, "but you've seen the projections. We will be next month. And all of our three-month trends are way up. Anyway, when I took this role there was no four-month window. It was one year, and I'm not even seven months in. We'll be well into the black by the time we hit the one-year time frame." I stood up and started pacing back and forth beside the conference room table. I had nervous and angry energy to spare. "Ralph, we've done significant things here. We've turned a money-loser into a money-maker. We're looking at adding a night shift, ramping things back up, bringing more jobs back to the community. You can't just throw all of that away." I gave him what I hoped was my most convincing in-charge look. "You're a business guy, Ralph, above all. It's simply good business to keep us going."

Ralph's expression wasn't giving anything away. "Why do you think I'm here?" he asked.

I stopped pacing and slumped into my chair. "To shut us down. Move things to Indonesia. Or just sell off the equipment and the plant and get right out of the business."

Ralph shook his head. "Wrong, Will. Sorry to disappoint you, but that's not what I came to talk about. At least, not quite."

I raised an eyebrow. "Then why fly out here? If you're going to give us more time, why not just talk to me about it on the phone?"

He raised an eyebrow right back at me. "You always think the worst of me, don't you, Will? You think I don't care about people."

"I've worked with you for, what, fifteen years, Ralph. I *know* that you don't care about people. You care about business."

Ralph put his hand over his heart. "Ouch, Will, that hurts. It really does." He smiled. "But fair enough. My responsibility is to the business, and sometimes that means I have to make tough decisions about people. That's what the shareholders and the board pay me to do. We're not running a charity here. Having said that, you're not running a charity here at Hyler, either, are you?"

"I'm not sure what you mean by that," I said. "Of course this isn't a charity. If you'd look at our numbers, you'd see that!" I wasn't doing a great job of moderating my voice.

Ralph held up his hands in mock surrender. "You're taking all the fun out of this, Will. I thought I could play you along for a while, but with you it's always cut to the chase. Listen, I'm out here in person for a few reasons. One is to say to you, face to face, that you've done a fantastic job in the last seven months. Seriously. You know I appreciate your skills, Will. I was sure you were wasting your time out here, but you dug into your little bag of tricks and pulled out a big rabbit. I give you my consent to say, 'I told you so,' but I really wouldn't recommend it."

I wasn't that stupid. I let Ralph keep talking.

"Will, you came out here for personal reasons. You had no way of knowing you could make this division viable, but you did. And for that I salute you. I offer you my sincere congratulations, and I want once again to offer you a job."

What was he on about, I wondered. "Thanks for the nice words, Ralph. But your mention of a job offer is confusing me. What's happening with Hyler? A minute ago I got the impression you were going to say you weren't closing us down. Now you want me to take a new job. What gives?"

Ralph sighed. "It's complicated, Will. Maybe I'd better back up a little and explain." He leaned back in his chair and made a show of looking around the conference room. "I have so many positive memories of this place. It's where I held my first executive position in the company. It's what launched me into Mantec. Without this place, there'd be no CEO title on my business card." I almost thought I could detect a hint of emotion in Ralph's voice, though I was sure I was mistaken. "But like you said, I'm all about business. Just because I like this place doesn't mean it makes sense for Mantec to own it."

"I knew it!" I interrupted loudly. "You never had any plans to keep Hyler. You were going to sell it all along. Well, why the hell did you let me come out here and spend the last seven months trying to make things work?"

Once again Ralph held up his hands in mock surrender. "Easy, boy, easy. I had no idea where we were going with Hyler when you convinced me to let you take this place over. If you will recall, I did try to talk you out of it. I believe I was pretty clear I didn't think there was a future here." He leaned forward and put his palms on the table. "For the record, however, I thought if anyone could make this place work, it would be you. What I didn't count on was the board taking such a keen interest in this operation."

"The board? What do they care about Hyler?"

"The board is interested in the shareholders, Will, and in getting the best return for them. They're even more about business than I am."

I nodded impatiently. "OK, so? What does the board want to do with this place?"

Ralph laced his fingers together and sat back. "At the board retreat three months ago, they decided that we should exit the consumer products business entirely. They want the corporation to focus more on the heavy industry sectors and the business-to-business stuff."

He looked me in the eye. "It's actually a good idea. Consumers are a funny bunch, and when you're exposed to their whims and tastes, it can make earnings more unpredictable than the shareholders would like. Especially when your other businesses include oil. So it wasn't actually a decision about Hyler, more about the direction of Mantec.

"Once that was decided, we had to make some choices about our business units. When it came to Hyler, the board asked me to put my best executive out here, turn the place around as quickly and as much as was possible, and then divest. I told them I'd get right on it." He chuckled, though I wasn't feeling amused. "Once more, Will, you are going to enhance my reputation as someone who can get things done. When the board sees what's happened at Hyler in the three months since the retreat, they're going to think I'm a genius. All thanks to you, of course."

I scowled. "Not that they'll ever hear that."

Ralph looked stern. "Will, you know better. I've always shared the credit. When one of my team does great work, everyone knows about it. It wouldn't be good business to do otherwise." I had to admit grudgingly that he had a point. Ralph was many things, but he had never been one to steal credit. He'd just been good enough or lucky enough to have team members who had done great stuff while they worked for him. And I guess when that happens over and over, you've got to acknowledge the leader of the team for putting those people in place.

"You're right, Ralph. I'm just feeling a little anxious."

"I get it," he said. "But there's nothing to be anxious about. It's just business, as you said. And that's why I'm here to chat with you. When the board sees what you've done, they're going to be very happy, and keen to approve you as my new chief operating officer."

I blinked. "What happened to Hugh?" Hugh McKillop was Mantec's current COO.

Ralph gave me a disgusted look. "You are not nearly political enough, Will. Even about the basics. How old do you think Hugh is?"

I hadn't really thought of that before. Based on how Hugh looked, and the fact that Ralph had inherited him from his predecessor, I was guessing not so young any more. "I assume he's not about to turn forty?"

Ralph laughed. "One hundred and forty, maybe. Hugh has been bugging me about succession for the last five years. He's ready to go. He's just waiting for someone we trust to step in and take over."

By now, most of my anger was gone, but I was still confused. "What makes you think my answer is going to be any different now than it was seven months ago, when you let me take this job?"

Ralph shrugged. "I wasn't offering you the COO role that time, Will. And given your age and my age, this isn't just about the COO position. This is about the chance to be CEO. You have to admit that would be an interesting move to cap your career. But forget about that, even. Do you have any idea what the COO of a multi-billion-dollar corporation makes these days?"

"What the hell are you talking about, Ralph? Did someone slip you some crystal meth on the plane out here?"

"Like I said, Will, you need to pay more attention to basic politics. Who has spent more time in more of our operations around the country and around the world than you? Who has had more success at solving sticky problems than you have? Who has been more committed to the organization, willing to go anywhere at the drop of a hat, do anything that's required in order to make things better? I mean, with the exception of me, of course."

I had to admit that some of what he was saying was true. "Well, Ralph, this is more than a little overwhelming. Ten minutes ago I thought you were in here to tell me we're closing the plant, and now you're putting divestment and the rest of this on the table."

He smiled. "Like I said, I wanted to surprise you."

"The surprise factor is apparently working," I said, "because I'm having a hard time processing all of this."

Things were about to get even more confused. My assistant Amy burst in the door. "Will, you need to call home. Like, right away."

I got a cold and prickly feeling down my spine. "Who called? Did they say what it's about?"

Amy nodded. "Your wife called. I guess it's her grandmother."

SIXTEEN

TRANSITIONS

ACCORDING TO JENNY'S mother, Martha hadn't woken up that morning at her regular time, and while I was starting my meeting with Ralph, Jenny's mom was calling an ambulance. By the time I got to the hospital, Martha was unconscious, breathing shallowly, and looking like she'd aged a hundred years since I last saw her.

We sat around her bed talking to her and each other, hoping the sound of familiar voices would bring her out of her coma-like state. But nothing seemed to make a difference. We kept talking, and Martha kept sleeping.

Around 2:00 p.m., the doctor asked us to step outside the room for a discussion. They weren't sure what was wrong with Martha, he told us, but at her age, he didn't expect a full recovery. Or any recovery at all, in fact. "She's lived such a long life," he said. "Her heart has probably pumped more than three billion times. Imagine." I knew he was trying to put things in a positive light, but his words sounded hollow and trite in that moment. We shuffled back into the room and continued our vigil.

I went out to get some sandwiches around 6:00 p.m., and when I came back, Jake summed things up perfectly. "This sucks," he said, sounding both tired and sad. "I mean, sure, she's 102 frickin' years old, and I guess we all gotta go sometime. But I just don't feel ready for it. G-squared's always been here. It's hard to imagine her gone."

Jenny was already misty-eyed, and when Jake stopped talking, she started full-on crying and hugged him. He must have been feeling emotional too, because he tolerated her hug much longer than normal.

By midnight, people had started dropping off to sleep, stretched out in various places around the room. Finally, just after 1:00 a.m., Jenny drifted off as well. I was left alone sitting beside Martha, thinking about her life and my place in it. I didn't feel tired or even sad at that point, just empty. I suppose deep down inside I was holding out hope that she would come out of her trance and we could have one last conversation, just the two of us. I would tell her about the weird turn of events with Ralph, and she could make fun of me but give me some sage advice about the whole thing. And help me figure out what to do next.

But that kind of thing happens only in the movies. Instead, there I was, frantically ringing the call bell when Martha finally took one last, shuddering breath, and the heart monitoring alarm started its plaintive tone. The nurses and a doctor responded very quickly, but reviving her wasn't an option; it was all over before most people in the room were awake. Next thing we knew we were standing in the parking lot staring at our car, talking absently about funeral arrangements and trying to work up the energy to go home.

THE FUNERAL was held the following Saturday. It was, as per Martha's wishes, a family-only affair. Her will had specified that she be cremated and her ashes placed prominently on the eldest surviving offspring's mantel so she could watch over the family, with the ashes passed on down the line as her children departed this world so she could continue keeping watch. Creepy as it sounds, it was a very Martha-like request.

By the time Sunday evening rolled around, I had to attempt a return to the here and now. Ralph had been great about giving me the week to think things over. Hyler was getting more valuable every day, and Mantec wasn't in any rush to start the divestiture process. "I'm sure you'll make the right decision, Will," he told me before he flew back to Chicago. "Just keep in mind all the great things we can do together at Mantec." I hadn't been back to the plant all week, but the whole place knew that Ralph had come and gone, and nothing had been announced, which was probably driving people nuts.

I hadn't told Jenny anything about my conversation with Ralph yet either. But since our family had been at the center of my return to Hyler, I knew I had to start there.

I sat her down at the kitchen table. "Honey, I have something I have to talk to you about. I didn't want to bring it up over the last week, with Martha and all, but we've got to talk about it soon."

Her answer couldn't have surprised me more. "I know, Will. Ralph was here at the house. He came by on his way to the airport on Friday. But you were so upset about Martha that I didn't want to talk to you until you were ready."

I closed my mouth, and then opened it again. "Ralph was here? Where was I?"

"Making funeral arrangements, taking long walks, going through your mourning process." She took my hand. "It's OK, honey, I know how hard this hit you. I was just giving you some space." I was feeling a little disoriented; I thought I was dealing with Martha's death just fine.

"Seriously, he was here?" I asked again. I couldn't think of anything else to say.

"Yes, Will, and it won't change if you ask again," Jenny said.

"What'd he want?" I asked.

"He said making the offer to you was really about making an offer to the whole family, and he wanted to do that in person."

I was stunned. "Seriously—"

Jenny cut me off. "Don't ask me again!"

"But he told you about the whole offer, including the chief operating officer thing?"

"Yes, all of that," Jenny said. "And also about how well Hyler is doing. How you really turned the place around. He even sounded sad that the board had decided to get out of the business, which I didn't think was possible for Ralph." She looked at me. "So, what do you want to do?"

So far, I had only planned how I was going to explain the situation to Jenny. I hadn't thought beyond that. "I don't know," I said. Brilliant, insightful—that's me.

What Jenny said next took me by surprise. "The way I see it, we actually have a couple of choices."

"We have choices?" I asked. "I thought there was only one choice."

"Don't be silly, Will. There are always choices. Just because Ralph offers you a big promotion that comes with a big paycheck doesn't mean you don't have other options."

"I kind of like being employed though, honey. It makes paying the mortgage so much easier."

She pulled a sour face. "Funny guy. Who says you couldn't just stay with Hyler?"

I frowned. "But you heard Ralph. Mantec is selling the plant."

"You don't think whoever buys it isn't going to want to keep the successful management team on?"

There were too many negatives in that sentence to parse it easily, but I thought I knew what she meant. "Well, yeah, I guess that's a possibility." I paused. "How long have I been with Mantec?"

"Forever," Jenny said. "But it's still an option, and Ralph figured it would be high on your list." Clearly, Ralph and my wife were way out in front of me on this one. As Martha would have been quick to point out, that was not unusual.

"What about taking the job?" I asked. "We'd have to move to Chicago. How do you feel about that?"

"We could make it work, Will. We've talked about moving before. It just never made sense." Jenny took my hand and looked me in the eyes. "I'm happy to support you, and so are the kids. I can work from anywhere, and they could learn to like a new school. Might even be good for them to have a change. They've had the same friends now since the first grade. The only condition I have is that you have to really want to do it. No going and then whining about it being a terrible mistake." She let go of my hands and got a more determined look. "In fact, no whining at all. That has to be part of the deal."

"RALPH THINKS WE'VE hit it out of the park." I looked around the faces at the conference table. The whole crew was there: Amanda, Luigi, Stu, Alice, Sheila, Mark. Leslie was, of course, noticeably absent.

"He thinks we've done a spectacular job. There's not a whole heck of a lot else to say."

Amanda was the first to speak. "So, what are you saying? He's not going to close us down?"

I shook my head. "Of course not. I can't believe you were worried about that!" I ducked as Amanda threw a pencil at me. "You guys have seen the results. We're trending in the right direction in pretty much every category. In another month we'll be profitable, and we'll finish the year in the black for the entire year. We're going to go ahead with adding a third shift, and we're going to spend some money on product development. It's all good."

Always the cynic, Stu said, "But?"

"But what?" I asked.

"But what's the catch, Will? I know you, and I know Ralph. You're hiding something, and with Ralph nothing is ever as straightforward as it seems. There's a catch here, and your crappy poker face is doing nothing to hide it. So give."

I looked around the table at the group. "ok, there's a 'but.'"

"I knew it!" said Sheila. She held out her hand to Mark, who took out his wallet and gave her a five-dollar bill.

"You guys are betting on the fate of this company?" I asked, feeling a little hurt.

Sheila smirked. "Oh, get over it, Will. We made a bet that you've been holding out on us, that's all."

Stu crossed his arms. "It's the scorpion's nature again, and in this case, Ralph is the scorpion."

"That's not really fair," I said. "Anyway, as we've demonstrated, it's not about 'nature,' it's about what gets rewarded. In our case, the rewarding going on at the corporate level will be a little different than we thought. It's called a change of direction."

"What does that mean?" Mark said.

"It means Hyler is no longer part of Mantec's strategic direction. Correction: consumer products in general are no longer part of Mantec's strategic direction. Since Hyler is exclusively a consumer products company, we're not part of that direction either."

The faces around the table looked surprisingly unconcerned. "To repeat," asked Sheila, "what does that mean? Although I'm pretty sure I can see where this is going."

"Mantec's board made this decision independent of Hyler's current performance. Our turnaround means they now have an asset that's worth a lot more than it once was. Their plan is to get the best deal they can while divesting themselves of consumer products."

Stu spoke up again. "Which translates to them selling Hyler, am I right?"

"You're right," I said.

"So all this hard work, the big turnaround we pulled off in the last seven months, that doesn't mean anything?" asked Amanda.

"No," I said, shaking my head. "I mean, yes. All our good work is still good work, and it still means something. When you think about it, it means a lot. We're much more likely to get bought by someone who really *wants* us, now that we're profitable again. Whether we were staying with Mantec or getting sold, what we've done in the last seven months has almost certainly saved Hyler. We're going to have new owners. That's all that's going to change. Our new owners are going to want us to keep growing and building and making the operation better. They're going to want to invest and expand and help us get to new levels of success. That's why they'll be buying Hyler."

Stu narrowed his eyes. "You used the word 'we' there. Did you mean it?"

I shifted uncomfortably in my chair. "I don't honestly know, Stu. Ralph made me an appealing offer, and I'm still thinking about it."

Part of me felt an embarrassing rush of satisfaction at how unhappy my confession made people look. The other part of me resented them for making me feel guilty for considering a job as COO in a Fortune 500 company rather than committing to Hyler.

Stu stood up. "Well, whatever you decide, Will, we know you're going to do whatever you find most reinforcing. And since that's what we all do, too, we can't be pissed off at you for it." He smiled and looked around the table. "Don't forget the performance model, guys. Remember the power of people avoiding unpleasant consequences. We all know how much Will would dread coming into this room to tell us he was leaving Hyler. How incredibly *guilty* that would make him feel. How *disappointed* we would all feel in him. How that would let us all down." He turned to me. "But no pressure, buddy, because like I said, you'll do what you need to do. You scorpion, you."

Each person around the table stood up and filed by me, shaking my hand.

"Guys," I protested, "I haven't left yet!"

Stu laughed. "You're right, Will. And we have no intention of letting that happen. All we need to do is make it so that the rewards you get from staying, combined with the avoidance of all the unpleasantness that goes with leaving, add up to more than whatever Ralph has offered. By now, we all know that drill."

Bastards! I couldn't believe they would turn all this crap against me!

SEVENTEEN

WILL THINKS ABOUT THE BIGGER IMPLICATIONS

THAT NIGHT, I saw Martha again. I'm pretty sure it was a dream, but it was so vivid to me the next morning that I wasn't 100 percent sure I hadn't received a visit from a ghost.

In my dream, I was standing at the edge of Lake Hyler, throwing stones into the water. The lake was almost impossibly calm, like a huge pane of dark glass lying on the ground. Each stone I threw created a small splash and then a series of perfect, concentric circles spreading into the distance.

"Scaring the ducks, are you, Willie?" a voice asked in my ear.

I turned to see Martha standing behind me. "You died," I told her.

She laughed and blew a smoke ring in my face. "Indeed I did, Willie, my boy. And I'll tell ya, it's not as easy as it looks." She brought her pipe up to her mouth and took another puff.

"What does that mean?" I turned around in a slow circle. "Is this real?"

Martha snorted. "Of course it is, Willie. And it's all in your head too."

Martha sat down in a rocking chair that I hadn't noticed on the grass behind her. "Now, what did you call me here for? I've got more important things to be doing. Death isn't some big vacation, you know."

I was feeling dazed, so I sat down on the chair that had suddenly materialized beside me. "I don't know," I said.

Martha shook her head. "Now, Willie, I don't get summoned for just anything. I'm only making the trip back because you've got some problem you need me to help solve. That's how it works with these things. Don't you read books anymore?"

She took another couple of puffs on her pipe. The smoke rings she blew quickly lost their circular shape and started looking like African animals. At least I thought they did. I shook my head. "Whoa," I said. "I missed out on a whole generation of crazy acid trips, but right now I feel like I'm on one."

Martha clicked her tongue. "Focus, young Willie, focus. Whether or not you understand the rules of these visitations, we have to abide by them. Let's figure out what you need so I can get back to where I was."

"And where was that, exactly?" I asked.

Martha took her pipe out of her mouth and wagged it back and forth at me. "Jeez, Willie, that is definitely *never* the purpose of these visits. I'm here to help you with your world, not tell you about what happens after the lights go out. So stay on point." She paused to blow another freaky smoke ring; this one turned into a galloping horse before it dispersed into nothingness. "I was under the impression we'd already dealt with your performance issue. Am I right?"

"How could you possibly know that?" I asked.

Martha smiled. "You were going down the path of adopting the Performance Principle. How could it work out any other way?"

I thought about it for a second. "Well, I guess since this is my dream, it makes sense you'd know about that."

Martha snorted. "Don't get all metaphysical on me, Willie Boy! It's not going to help anyone. Let's get to the nub of the question. Think on it, Willie, think."

I seemed to have lost the power to think about anything without words coming out of my mouth, which I suppose is appropriate in a dream. "Yes...no...yes, we dealt with the biggest of Hyler's performance issues. The plant is in the black, and we're applying the Performance Principle across most departments now. It's catching on like wildfire and making a huge difference in just about all aspects of how Hyler works. People love it because it helps them understand what makes things work well. It's amazing how reinforcing simply *understanding* something can be.

"My problems have changed, though. Even though Hyler is performing, Mantec is getting out of the consumer products business, and we're the biggest piece of that. Now I've got to decide whether I want to stick with Hyler through the sale or become the COO of Mantec."

Martha laughed. "Indeed, Willie. That's called life, isn't it? You solve what you think is your biggest problem, and then life turns around and hands you something else entirely. Sets you on your ass again, and you have to learn to walk all over. It's kind of funny that way."

Martha paused, and we both gazed out over the impossibly smooth water of the lake. "Do you know what you're gonna do?" she asked me finally.

"Not yet, but I'm pretty sure that's not why I called you here." I looked at her and squinted. "If I actually did call you here."

Martha made an impatient noise. "I don't have all day, Willie. If that isn't what you wanted to talk about, well then, what is?"

I picked up another rock and threw it far out into the lake. "I guess it's because this whole Performance Principle thing has got me disturbed."

Martha looked perplexed. "Disturbed? How exactly?"

"It's the implications of the model. They kind of freak me out."

Martha grinned. "Oh, that kind of disturbed."

"So you know what I'm talking about?" I asked.

Martha laughed. "Oh, I know what you're talking about. Don't think I didn't spend some time early on wondering about the larger meaning of the whole thing myself."

My dream self was flooded with a deep relief. "I get how the model works to describe people's behaviors, and it really helps when you're setting things up to get the results you want. But what about the moral implications of doing all that?"

"Willie, there are no moral implications. You're not asking people to do something they wouldn't do otherwise. And you're being completely open with them about the process. Everyone understands what's going on. You set things up so people understand how to get what they want and are able to do it." She looked at me closely, then blew a smoke ring in my face, just like old times.

"But we've already had this conversation, so that's not what you mean by 'moral implications,' is it?"

I shuffled my feet uncomfortably. "No. I mean, I'm not talking about some kind of mind control, or about getting people to do things they wouldn't normally do. I'm talking about something bigger than that. Hell, I guess I mean the question of whether people have any free will in the first place!" I was almost shouting by the end of my last sentence. I suddenly felt as if I was talking too loudly in a library, and I looked around to see if someone was going to shush me. "Am I violating the etiquette of the dead here, Martha, by getting too excited?"

Martha looked at me slyly. "I have no idea what you're talking about, Willie Boy. This is *your* dream."

She hopped up from her rocking chair as if she was eighteen years old.

I stared at her. "How can you move like that?"

Martha ignored me. "You're struggling with what I think of as the next layer of the Performance Principle, Willie. It's a place we all end up if we ponder it long enough, and it can be troublesome. Societies in the developed world, particularly in North America, are preoccupied with the belief that the individual is king. That the individual has the power to decide what he or she is going to do. That we have independent free will and the ability to make all of our own choices." Martha stooped to pick up a rock. She hurled it across the water as if she was Willie Mays in center field throwing out a runner at home plate. "The Performance Principle lays out clearly why people do the things we do. We do them because we find them reinforcing or because we want to avoid punishment, and we stop doing things when reinforcement is removed. So what does the term 'selfish' really mean?"

"That's it!" I yelled. "If you accept the tenets of the Performance Principle, then we're all selfish! There's no such thing as an unselfish act. People who give to charity or work in a soup kitchen to help the homeless are doing those things because they find them rewarding. No one does something they hate every minute of unless they're doing it to avoid an unpleasant consequence like, say, jail time. By definition, then, there is no such thing as an unselfish act."

Martha was looking at me unblinkingly, with an expression of irritation. "Do you know what a rhetorical question is, Willie? I was asking you one of those. But thanks for answering it anyway." She laughed. "You're absolutely right. Selfish and unselfish are convenient and almost arbitrary constructs. They likely evolved because we human beings find the concept of free will so reinforcing. Santa Claus has similarly well-meaning origins, but that doesn't mean he's real, either."

Martha sat back down in her rocking chair, and suddenly she was holding a beer I hadn't noticed before. "Next time, could you bring something a little more exotic than lite beer?" she asked. She took a swig. "Anyway, the concepts of selfishness and unselfishness are part of an even more fundamental question, aren't they?"

I hesitated. "Are we fully into the Socratic method now? Is that a real question or a rhetorical one?" Martha waved her beer at me, which I interpreted as encouragement to continue. "The answer is yes, I think. The bigger question is, do we have any say at all in this thing we call life? We do what is reinforcing or will help us to avoid punishment. We're slaves to rewards. How can we conceive an original thought if we do only what's reinforcing? Thinking is really just talking to yourself, which means it's just another behavior, dictated by the rules of the Performance Principle. How can we step outside the model and exercise free will to determine what we want to change, and then change it? The way the model works, it doesn't seem like that's possible. We're caught in a feedback loop and we have no control. Because we only do whatever we need to do to get the next reward."

Martha nodded wisely. "Interesting questions, aren't they? Can the machine become self-aware?" She took a long draw on her pipe. "You're right, by the way. Most people agree that it's practical to think about self-talk as a behavior. It meets the criteria of being measurable, although individuals are the only ones who can observe it." She blew another animated smoke ring, and this time it formed the image of a man running in circles. Or maybe that was just my Rorschach interpretation based on how I was feeling. "If self-talk is behavior, then how we think fits into the Performance Principle model too. So—how can we possibly develop a new or different idea, or go forward with a series of actions that aren't the most immediately reinforcing thing on our behavioral menu at a particular moment? That's the real conundrum, isn't it? Do we have any *choice* in the matter at all? Or are we simply the product of what we find reinforcing?"

It was mind-boggling to consider. "So the only reason I'm not a raging alcoholic is that my body just doesn't find drinking all that reinforcing? And if that wasn't the case, I'd have no choice in the matter...?" My voice trailed off as I considered just how randomly assigned our lives might be. It was more complicated than that, but I imagined little robots with preprogrammed reinforcers trundling off the assembly line. Could the only reason I was with my wife, whom I consider the love of my life, be that I hadn't found someone more reinforcing? That sounded horrible.

"You're probably wondering about things like love, too, aren't you, Willie?" Martha continued. She laughed at my expression.

"But consider this: people who are alcoholics quit drinking. People who are in bad marriages get divorced. People who hate their jobs quit them. If we have no free will, how does all that work?"

I wasn't sure. "I guess, if you look through the lens of the model, either something about what someone is doing becomes so punishing that they change, or something else becomes a more powerful reinforcer. At some point, your crappy job becomes so punishing that getting paid isn't enough reinforcement to keep you in it. In your unhappy marriage, a similar thing happens, or someone new and more reinforcing comes along, outweighing whatever you were getting out of your marriage."

"Or whatever you were avoiding by not getting divorced," Martha added. "Yes, that's the logical explanation. Things do change, Willie. We are capable of considering other versions of the Performance Principle for ourselves. The question becomes, can we construct a new pattern that is more powerful than the current one? The real challenge is that many of the self-development things we want to do require us to get reinforcement from *deferring* reinforcement. Instead of eating that delicious doughnut every morning for breakfast, we take pleasure in going for a workout and thinking about how great we'll feel when we lose thirty pounds. Instead of that oh-so-delicious hit of nicotine," here she paused to take a long draw on her pipe, "the smoker thinks of the health benefits of quitting smoking—avoiding lung cancer and the like. In effect, people create their own reinforcements through more complex thought patterns and self-talk. But you know the problem with that, don't you, Willie?"

I thought I did. "It's damn hard to make future rewards more reinforcing than the immediate gratification from a doughnut. Or a cigarette. Or a Big Mac. Some people might say it's impossible."

Martha gave me a thumbs-up. "But people achieve that, don't they, Willie? They do it all the time. How?"

"Well, maybe they join groups of other people trying to make changes. They can help reinforce each other, or more likely, remind each other of the negative consequences of backsliding and doing whatever bad-but-oh-so-great-feeling thing they're trying to avoid." The prospect worried me a bit, because I've never really considered myself a support group kind of guy.

"ok," Martha said. "But that's just one way. How do you think your sales team felt at first when you imposed a new rewards scheme on them?"

I didn't hesitate. "They hated it."

"Right. And so why, Willie Boy, would you expect that making any change is going to be easy? Change requires us to break out of existing patterns of behavior, reward, and avoidance that are often complex. Why should that be easy?"

That sounded like another rhetorical question to me. Martha continued, "Understanding what drives our behavior gives us more of this thing we think of as freedom. What we have to do is recognize that and work with it. If we want to change things, why tackle the change in a way that's destined to fail while upholding our misunderstanding of free will? It isn't as simple as just choosing to do something different. To be successful, we first need to recognize *why* we're doing what we do. That doesn't mean we are any less free to choose our course."

"It sounds like a cliché, but nothing worthwhile is ever easy," I suggested.

"If you think about it," Martha said, "many of the homilies we spout actually have their roots in an understanding of the Performance Principle. It may not be framed in quite the same way, but it's there nonetheless."

We sat quietly for a moment while I considered Martha's words. She broke the silence. "Are you disappointed there's not some easy way out, Willie?"

"Yes," I had to agree. "I guess I am. But what you're saying has a certain sense to it."

Martha stood up from her chair. "Remember something else, too, Willie. There's no one answer to everything. The Performance Principle is another mental perspective, another tool in the toolbox. Use it wisely, but not exclusively."

Martha started walking toward the edge of the lake, which alarmed me. "Where are you going?" I asked her.

She turned to face me. "Our time here is done, Willie. It's my grand exit from your crazy dream." She turned back to the lake and waded into the water.

"Wait!" I called. "You haven't answered my other big question!" She swung around to face me once more. "You know," I said, "about the job. What should I do?"

Martha smiled at me. "Whatever you find most reinforcing." She took two more strides and then dove into the lake and disappeared.

"WILL! WILL!" The voice was calling to me from somewhere in the distance. "Will, honey, wake up! Wake up!" The voice came nearer, and I realized that someone was shaking me. I opened my eyes. It was Jenny. "Will, wake up. You're going to be late for work."

I nodded groggily. "I'm awake, I'm awake. What time is it?"

"Seven fifteen. When you didn't get up with the alarm, I thought you must be tired, but I never expected you to sleep this late."

I sat up in bed. "I was having the weirdest dream."

"About the job offer?" Jenny asked.

"No. Well, sort of. It was about Martha. She was visiting me. At Hyler."

Jenny smiled sadly. "I still can't believe she's gone." She pointed to my bedside table. "Hey, I didn't know you had that."

I turned to look where she was pointing. There sat Martha's pipe. "That's weird. I didn't know I had it either." I picked it up. Warm ash spilled out of the bowl and onto the sheets.

"Watch out!" Jenny said. "Were you smoking that thing?"

I shook my head as I brushed away the ashes. "I'm not exactly sure, honey. I'm not exactly sure."

GLOSSARY

BEHAVIOR—An observable activity undertaken by an individual or a group.

CONSEQUENCE—What happens to a person (the performer) as a result of a behavior.

EXTINCTION—The removal of a positive consequence for a behavior. Intended to decrease the occurrence of a behavior.

LEAN MANUFACTURING (LEAN)—A systematic method for the elimination of waste within a manufacturing system by focusing only on creating "value," which is defined as any action or process that a customer would be willing to pay for. There are varying perspectives on how this is achieved. Lean manufacturing is a management philosophy derived mostly from the Toyota Production System and identified as "Lean" only in the 1990s.

LEARNING HISTORY—The sum of a person's past behaviors and consequences.

NEGATIVE REINFORCEMENT—The removal or avoidance of a negative or aversive consequence as a consequence of a behavior. Example:

Fred drives the speed limit (behavior) in order to avoid getting a ticket (negative consequence).

POSITIVE REINFORCEMENT—A reward or positive consequence following a behavior. Increases the likelihood that the behavior will occur again in the future.

PUNISHMENT—An aversive or negative (to the person or performer) consequence that occurs as an outcome of a behavior.

RESULT—The outcome of a behavior. It can affect others as well as the person performing the behavior.

SIX SIGMA—A set of tools and techniques used to improve processes. The Greek letter sigma is used in statistics to represent standard deviation, or the amount of variation in a set of data. The term is derived from the application of statistics to the process of improving quality in manufacturing processes with the goal of producing zero defects. Motorola is credited with first applying the Six Sigma concept to process improvement broadly, in many cases including processes that had not previously been measured using statistical tools. General Electric adopted Six Sigma as well, and it subsequently became popular in the mainstream business community. As with Lean, practitioners receive training in the approach and methods. They receive colored belt designations based on their level of certification, culminating in a license to kill... to kill waste, defects, and poor customer satisfaction, that is.

STATISTICAL QUALITY CONTROL/STATISTICAL PROCESS CONTROL (SPC)— The use of statistical methods to improve the quality of a given process. SPC is a generic term applied to a variety of statistical techniques used to improve quality. Terms such as "continuous improvement" and "elimination of defects or waste" are commonly associated with SPC.

STIMULUS—Anything that provides an occasion for a behavior to take place.

TOTAL QUALITY MANAGEMENT (TQM)—A term used to refer to a company-wide or organization-wide initiative to permanently establish a culture of seeking continuous improvement. Unlike Six Sigma or Lean, there is no single agreed-on approach, but TQM efforts typically draw on statistical process control methods. TQM enjoyed widespread attention during the late 1980s and early 1990s before being overshadowed by ISO 9000, Lean, and Six Sigma.

ACKNOWLEDGMENTS

THE ORIGINS of this book are difficult to trace with precision. Starting with my formal introduction to B. F. Skinner in a second-year psychology course taught by Dr. Loren Acker at the University of Victoria, the conversation about what drives human behavior has occupied much of my working life. Many individuals have contributed their knowledge, perspective, and wisdom over the years, but special thanks are due to a few: my father, whose unique take on this and other things has been invaluable in all aspects of my life; Dr. Judy Agnew and later Dr. Bruce Hesse, higher-order researchers and practitioners in this field; my sons, Aidan and Nicolas, who have taught me more than anyone about the practical elements of understanding human behavior; and my wife, Laura, whose support in all aspects of writing this book has been invaluable and unwavering, and who forms the most important part of the learning history of my life.

MACKENZIE KYLE has more than 25 years' experience in operations and process improvement, and he has provided specific assistance in everything from strategic planning and performance management to managing projects. He focuses on assisting clients to identify and implement strategic change and improve team performance, providing a unique approach that bridges the gap between theory and the practical application of technique.

He has worked in a variety of industries in Canada, the U.S., Australia, New Zealand, and Asia, including manufacturing, transportation, and telecommunications, as well as in the public sector. He is currently the managing partner for MNP for the Greater Vancouver region as well as for MNP's advisory services team in British Columbia. MNP is one of Canada's leading national accounting, tax, and consulting firms.

Mackenzie's first book, *Making It Happen: A Non-technical Guide to Project Management*, has sold more than forty thousand copies. He has developed a series of tools to help organizations and individuals with performance management, project management, and organizational improvement. Mackenzie offers consulting services as well as specialized training programs, and he is a regular speaker on these and related topics. He welcomes inquiries and can be contacted at mackenzie.kyle@mnp.ca.